The Wait

Finding peace and waiting well in the eye of the storm

Lucy West

Equipping the Church

First published 2023 by Equipping The Church

British Library Cataloguing-in-Publication Data

A catalogue record for this book is available from the British Library.

Photo by Szabo Viktor on Unsplash

ISBN: 978-1-80376-014-8

Printed in the UK

What Others Are Saying...

Remarkable for its honesty and raw vulnerability – no sugar coating here! While Lucy's own story is about infertility and waiting for a baby, the book she's written is actually relevant to any of us experiencing personal pain, whatever it may look like.
Revd Canon Archie Coates. Vicar, Holy Trinity Brompton

This is such a helpful book, addressing the silent pain of childlessness and the complex joy. Lucy writes honestly and with wonderful warmth. I'm quite sure that her story is going to bring comfort and hope to many, many people.
Pete Greig, 24-7 Prayer International

The pain of infertility can be almost unbearable and often very difficult to talk about. I am delighted that Lucy West has written this book to encourage others that they are not alone and that there is hope along the journey.
Nicky Gumbel

Lucy has courageously shared hers and Lindz's precious story of hope and heartbreak at becoming parents. It's something that so many of us take for granted. Lucy's honesty will shock some but comfort others and hopefully educate some who are oblivious to what couples go through on their parenting journey. This isn't just a book for those who can empathise but really is a book to help people sympathise; it offers insight, understanding, suggestions and mostly, hope. I am so proud of my friend for sharing something so incredibly personal and stand with her in solidarity for this lovingly supporting everyone who needs it.
Gemma Hunt

We've long admired our friends Lucy and Lindz for the way they've navigated their story of starting a family. After reading Lucy's wonderful new book, we admire them even more. In *The Wait* we're invited deep inside their journey – from infertility through to adoption. Along the way are many raw emotions, agonising prayers and painful questions. Yet running through it all is a thread of hope and their faith in God – and ultimately this is a redemptive story. This is a powerful read and will help many!

Matt and Beth Redman

Contents

Foreword

When I was asked to write the foreword for Lucy's book, I saw it as a significant honour. Let me explain why. There are few people I would agree to do a book foreword for, not just because I'm insanely busy, but because there are few books on this topic delivered from a place of humility and quiet contemplation. There also aren't many faith-based books on the topic of infertility that don't end with a biological child in one's arms, and I think we need to read stories like these, as the dialogue around this subject can often be 'pray harder and you will get your heart's desire'... but that's not everyone's story.

There are two types of foreword for a book. The first is a brief description of the content and an endorsement that people should read it. Then there is the foreword which I, as a reader, appreciate way more – one that wholeheartedly endorses the writer. When choosing a book, I want to know about the person who crafted each word; I want to know their character speaks louder than the words on the page. So that's what I will be writing here.

Lucy is kind, thoughtful, dynamic, humble, and deeply believes in Jesus. While journeying through infertility, her faith appears to have gotten stronger rather than weaker, and that's beautiful to witness. Instead of running from the pain, she has learned to lean into it and bravely ask herself and Jesus vital questions.

Having navigated heartbreak and loss myself, I dislike stories that try to make everything pretty. You know, the ones where you hear of such sadness and trauma, but through prayer and commitment all becomes right. The narrative concludes by presenting a beautifully wrapped gift with a bow on the top. Many people's stories aren't as neat as that. Many tragically don't get a happy ending, and some have to adjust their life choices to accommodate the pain and grief and look for different life paths.

Lucy so wonderfully explains her challenging walk and shows how she has found great hope and joy from travelling an unexpected trail, she never expected she would need to take.

Sadly, our faith doesn't stop us from journeying through hard things. Oh, how I wish it did, but it doesn't! But what we can do is surround those who are navigating grief, loss and challenging circumstances with love and support, so they don't feel alone on their walk.

One of the ways in which we can do this is by bravely sharing our personal stories, so that when others are feeling isolated and like they are the only person in the world feeling what they do (which most people experiencing infertility and loss do feel), they can see that others have journeyed these paths and, more importantly, have survived them. These essential stories become beacons of hope; they are the lighthouses in the darkness and they give people hope to continue.

In 'The Wait' Lucy shares this:

> "During this time, I came to the very painful conclusion that the 'ticking clock' feeling I was experiencing was very real and very painful when left unfulfilled. It's like having a time of grieving with nothing to show for your grief. There was no guarantee that Lindz and I would ever be parents. There was no fixed date in the future when we knew these clouds would clear. It was like walking in the wilderness with no clear path or signs to follow, no boundaries and no finish line. Being in the wilderness can bring a deep exhaustion, as you have nothing to help you navigate. You feel isolated and forgotten, like your life has been put on pause while everyone else's moves on. The dictionary definition of

> 'wilderness' speaks of a 'neglected or abandoned area'; a place that is 'uncultivated, uninhabited and inhospitable'. It's an accurate description of the place we found ourselves in. With no end in sight, every one of my senses told me that I was going to feel this way forever."

Lucy's words accurately describe what so many women and men feel – they are genuinely navigating the wilderness – and simply knowing you aren't alone in these feelings can be a gift to the soul.

One of the treasures you will discover in this book is Lucy's perspective on navigating unplanned paths and how the most unexpected journeys can lead to the most beautiful places. You will also hear how these painful life events can sometimes bring with them the greatest of rewards, and how the desires of one's heart can sometimes be delivered in ways you never considered possible.

So, who is this book for? Well, it's a story for anyone experiencing infertility. This book will become an excellent companion on your walk. But please don't feel this book is not for you if you *haven't* experienced these challenges. Read this book to gain a greater understanding of the world of infertility and faith; read this to educate yourself on a rarely discussed subject, so you can be an even better friend or a supportive family member.

Thank you, Lucy (and Lindz), for baring your soul to the world and being vulnerable with your pain. So many people will be grateful that you trusted them with your story. I will end with one of my quotes which I feel is so apt:

> "We aren't supposed to know what to do; we are meant to feel our way in the darkness. As we explore, we discover that the beauty lies in the hidden locations, in the unexpected rooms, in the

places we would have never entered if we hadn't been lost in the first place."

Zoe Clark-Coates MBE, Grief Specialist, CEO, TV Presenter and Government Advisor

Acknowledgements

There have been many people who have helped me in the writing of this book – from the support and wisdom we were given during our journey, to the practical help of how to actually create the finished product.

Thank you to Jamie Hill, Mat Owen and Ian O'Reilly, for believing in the book in the first place. Thank you Zoe (Clark-Coates) for constantly encouraging me that there was a book inside me, and showing me how to reach the end and keep on going! Thank you to some wonderful women who either spoke life into me or helped me to see the structure my book needed to take. Katie Levell, Debra Green, Ems Hancock, you helped get my thoughts in line. Tim Pettingale, your editing and knowledge has really helped to take my book through the final hurdles to get me here…into print! Thank you to those who took the time to read through my manuscript and write a beautiful endorsement, I so appreciate all of you.

Thank you to those who walked with us all those years; those who just put their arms around us, fed us, and checked in on us when everyone else had disappeared. The Clarks, Lamberths, Hawthornes and Delaneys especially, we love you. An extra special thank you to our wonderful friend, Dave Clark. When we lost you, we all lost an incredible support; a friend who had become family and one of our biggest cheerleaders. There is still a hole where you should be, but I will be eternally grateful you were there with us for so long, constantly encouraging us to be better and push deeper, and loving us so well.

The biggest thank you needs to go to my wonderful husband and the children who filled that awful ache we were feeling. Lindz, you walked the same journey but saw things so differently to me. You continued to stay positive, you continued to support me as I melted into nothing, and you have continued to pull me out of any bumps I may still trip or stumble over every now and again. I love you. Jack and Willow, our chosen children. We believe with everything in us that you were our Plan A – that God had you lined up for us since the beginning of time. Our timing didn't match up with God's, but we can see now you were always ours, however long we had to wait. You are SO loved.

Prologue

There she was again, in the corner of the room, rocking backwards and forwards, hugging her knees tightly to her chest. Wracking sobs made the strangest of noises as they escaped from her mouth. She wouldn't move from this spot until all her crying was done for the day. Then, she would go through life once more, pretending to those she met that all was fine. The relief of knowing that she had the time and space for this silent screaming – all alone for now – helped her to relax into her desperately sad, pitiful role. This girl in the corner was barely recognisable from the happy-go-lucky, maybe a little naïve, girl who had loved till it hurt and cried at the slightest sign of a happy ending or show of emotion. This is who I had become, slowly, over the course of a few years; a few deeply painful years of waiting and trying for children. In my corner I felt like I was outside of myself, looking down on a mess of a human being. Who was this person? This wasn't me was it?

I certainly didn't choose this for myself. I had grown up in a home surrounded by children. I adored children and always believed I would have a football team of them. So, how was I now in such a difficult place of anguish? Not only had I watched my sister walk this difficult path year after year, but now I was suffering the same fate.

Infertility.

How does it affect you? The best way I can describe it is that it dismantles you bit by bit… your dreams, your self-worth, your friendships, sometimes your finances, your marriage or relationship, and so much more. And at the age when you have to walk through it, these are some of the most important things keeping your life afloat.

Thoughts of legacy and a healthy family tree frighteningly seem to disappear before your eyes. The dawning realisation that you may be the last of your line, your genes never to be intertwined and replicated with the person you so love; forever a stump instead of a blossoming tree. Shame begins to take root when you realise your body can't do the seemingly easiest of functions; one that billions of women over the years have managed without a thought. It's even written in the Bible as clear as day: "Go forth and multiply" (Genesis 1:28). But I couldn't and it was killing me.

On the whole, society still understands so little about infertility. Often, people feel a sense of awkwardness around those without children. Maybe they think, "What goes around comes around. Maybe it's karma. Perhaps they've spoken something over themselves, left it too late, done something wrong…" Or, "They probably damaged their bodies when they were younger and now it's come back to bite them on the bum." Perhaps even, "Maybe their relationship is bad and they're not sleeping together enough" or the devastating, "They're probably just not cut out to be good parents. It wasn't meant to be."

It's extraordinary how quick others are to make judgements. Even hospitals and IVF clinics can be a little blasé: "I'm sorry this is what is happening to you. Sorry the treatment didn't work. Bye, have a nice day…" and suddenly you are left with a huge, gaping chasm that your dreams for the future used to occupy and you have no idea how to fill.

I used to have days where I'd shake and cry at the thought of Christmas Day, with just the two of us as we got older. Fear gripped me when I imagined a silent dinner table with no laughter, no burps, no mess; no discussions about why dinosaurs can't be pets, how Wonder Woman's invisible plane works, or why the planet Uranus sounds so funny! My wonderful husband, Lindz, used to console me, reminding me that we have lots of friends and family who would be happy to spend Christmas with us, but it wasn't the same. I wanted to do it with *our* kids, *our* noise, *our* mess.

Then there was the shame…

This became a faithful friend to me over the years. Why do women and men feel ashamed about not having children? Goodness, I wish I had the answer to that one. I believe it is something that has been deeply embedded in society since the start of the human race, something we naturally pick up on. What I know for sure is that shame brings silence, and silence brings a deep loneliness that aches and aches.

Alongside this is the feeling that no one, absolutely no one, understands what you are walking through. People may come close and try to share anecdotes or encouraging stories they've heard about other people – their friend's Auntie's cousin at work – who has been on a similar journey, but few understand that ache; the vast wilderness of unanswered questions about the future.

Plus, how could I begin to tell people how deeply I was failing on the inside, when my life looked fine from the outside? The truth was, I was *kind of* fine. For Lindz and me, life carried on as normal and we *did* look okay – so how were we supposed to feel then? Was it simply a case of "life goes on, get over it"? How could I suppress the ache of my biological clock, ticking away, or ignore the monthly cramps that teased me in the midst of my pain, a stark reminder of what my body should be doing.

What I did next, how I felt, and how together we dealt with this huge elephant in the room – that is what I am going to try and share with you.

Chapter One

The greatest fear in the world is that you're not going to fit in, you're not going to belong.
–Kris Vallotton

Children have always been a huge part of my life. I grew up in a rambling old rectory in the country, where it wasn't always easy to see friends or have a vibrant social life, but the surroundings were nonetheless beautiful and peaceful. Over the course of 30 years, our family fostered 107 children and young adults and adopted two, so our home was always full of noise, fun, and a "get your hands dirty and your heart broken" kind of love. Lindz grew up with his two brothers in a busy, noisy, love-filled family home in Maidenhead. He regularly took himself into London to socialise and had friendship groups on his doorstep.

When we got married, we decided to move to Wythenshawe, one of the poorest wards in the whole of the UK, into a home we felt the two of us were bursting out of – though most of our neighbours occupied the same size of home, often sharing it with six or seven people. It felt right to be there, and we knew we were giving back to society through a project called Eden. When we looked out of those rain covered windows at the grey, bleak view, however, there were times when we couldn't help wondering what on earth we were doing there.

There were regular knocks on our door, and we had many chats on our doorstep with young people who had nowhere to go that evening. I loved that they felt able to come, and that for a while they would be safe from harm, chatting away about make-up, boys, school – the normal things. But at times I also felt put-out and cold, my thoughts straying to all the things I needed to get done inside the house. Safeguarding policies made it necessary for us to keep young people talking on our doorstep, but I often felt a little mean that we couldn't just invite them in and give them a soft sofa and a bit of TV; a brief respite from their siblings and the fighting and chaos they often lived with.

Lindz was in a band, the Tribe, who for many years had travelled around the UK and Europe. They performed to huge crowds of happy people, who would sing their lyrics and join in with the actions, which generally made everyone very sweaty. He had recently taken the place of Cameron, and stepped right into his shoes, running up walls and back-flipping, much to the delight of those watching. Needless to say, his antics were part of the reason I had no trouble falling in love with this beautiful blondie. That, and an insane gift for parallel parking!

Lindz had also worked in a lot of local schools, meaning that he got recognised everywhere he went. I was often labelled "the other woman" i.e. the one who stood in the way of a young girl and her infatuation! I remember the angry looks I got when Lindz once announced at a gig that, "My beautiful wife is here watching." I advised him to maybe not say that in future, or I might get beaten up! In time, the Tribe sadly finished, but the band became LZ7 when Lindz realised it wasn't time for him to come off the stage just yet. Music has become his longest adventure so far and one that has grown larger and larger, stretching over continents and taking him to New Zealand, Australia, America and further. There aren't many places he hasn't visited and the masses of colourful fridge magnets we've collected over the years testify to these travels as soon as you lay eyes on them.

My work also brought me face to face with many children and young people. I trained at Plymouth University as a Primary school teacher and found my voice while I was there. I joined a band and began the nerve-wracking adventure of performing in small venues, pubs, clubs and churches. My confidence didn't match my voice to begin with, and looking back, singing and dancing in public (in fact, generally being in front of other people) was terrifying to me at the start. This first taste was enough, however, and I was determined to keep going. I auditioned for another band which put me in front of about 4,000 people on our first gig, and got me on stage performing dance routines – something I never dreamed I would do.

Sadly, this venture was short-lived and soon after I found myself in Manchester, when manager and songwriter Mark Pennells asked me to come and set up the band V*enna, which he and producer Zarc Porter wanted to send over to the US. Musically, it was going to be a mixture of Steps and Britney Spears with Abba-style harmonies and I bit their hands off to be involved, moving up to Manchester in the new year, ready for my next adventure. For the next 17 or so years, I sang and danced in three different bands, being slapped back into reality by doing supply teaching in some of the roughest school in Manchester in between each one. I would be chomping at the bit for something different to do, then another opportunity would come my way, which took me back to my ultimate love of singing. It was doing this, plus some help from the people I was living with, that brought me and Lindz together – something I will ALWAYS be grateful for!

Our different experiences had given us both a love for children and when we were about 28 years old, Lindz and I decided to "officially" start trying for our own – a funny way of talking about something we'd been up to for years before then, ha! We had been married for four years and our love was exciting – a relationship that seemed to go on a daily adventure. Now, we were about to set out on the craziest adventure of them all.

People warn you that your life will be very different once you have children, but is anyone really prepared for how different "different" really is? I don't think so. However, I felt ready. I was in BlushUK and my bandmates, Nic and Jess, were such a support to me and we felt like family. I was sure this would work out. I dreamt of being like Mel from All Saints, performing with a huge bump in clothes that enhanced it, rather than making her look huge or exhausted (which I'm sure she must have been at times). Then, I imagined coming into the rehearsal room with our little one, dressed in cool little trainers and dance clothes, and teaching them a bit of breakdancing before getting on with our rehearsals, while he or she played quietly in the corner with their toys (isn't that what babies do?!)

I love taking photos, so I imagined photographing our baby in lots of beautiful arty ways. Wrapping them up in a soft blanket, using all kinds of Photoshop magic to make them look as though they were sitting perfectly; propping their head up, folding their hands. And, of course, I would capture that perfect picture of their dinky little feet. These images would line the walls of our home for all to see when they came to visit. I dreamt up ways to keep the house tidy while my hormones were crashing around me. I thought of names we would call our little ones and about the colour and décor of the nursery.

What would that first meeting with our baby feel like? Lindz would be crying and I would be exhausted but overwhelmed with happiness. We would take that first selfie of us all and post it on Instagram, possibly later regretting it, due to the overshare of post-birth sweatiness! But our happiness would be evident for all to see. We would be parents!

I guess, like a young girl dreaming of one day getting married and all that day would bring, I allowed myself to dream about our children. Would they have blonde hair and an amazing figure like Lindz? Maybe they would have my blue eyes that often got me compliments instead of my "kankles" or "sturdy" figure and "heavy bones"! What would their characters be like? I dreamed of the personality traits they could inherit that would rocket them successfully into life, and about the traits I wouldn't miss if they didn't have them.

At this point in the dreaming process we never once thought that having children might be a difficult process. Around this time, my sister was trying to have children and was waiting to conceive. Naïvely, I suppose I thought that it was because she and her husband weren't having enough "sexy time", or maybe just at the wrong times of the month. I truly believed it would just be a matter of time before she announced her good news, and I was going to be right behind her. But six months later nothing had happened, and a new sensation started to niggle at me. Something didn't feel right. Lindz and I were both incredibly good with kids and had always wanted our own. And after all the children my family had cared for, surely we'd have no problem having our own?

What followed, over the next eight years, can only be described as a bittersweet journey, during which a process of deep suffering finally brought out incredible changes in us. During this time, we began to identify deeply with the process gold must go through to become the precious metal we know and love. Gold is "refined by fire", which means exposing it to an incredible amount of stress as it is melted down in temperatures of up to 1,000 degrees Celsius. As it breaks down, the impurities or "dross" rise to the surface and are skimmed off, until only pure gold is left.

We felt like a LOT of dross came to the surface of our lives during that time, but now we can honestly say we are so glad we went through it, because we have become stronger in our marriage, stronger in our faith, and stronger people in general. We now know that we will never process pain in quite the same way ever again. This was the pain that crept up on us, winded us, and beat us black and blue as it reached new depths and threw different agonising scenarios into our paths. But each time we fell, we got back up and carried on. Now we know that pain doesn't have to kill us. Like the saying, it can actually help to make us stronger. Importantly, having experienced it also enables us to help others make it through their suffering.

After a year or so of not being able to conceive, we decided to look more seriously into why nothing was happening. By doing so, we stepped into a minefield of questions and suffering we had no idea was out there. Even the most cursory search on the internet revealed so many people in so much pain. There were forums full of desperate people looking for answers, searching for ways to end their agonising journey of waiting. We had read that a 1-2-year wait was pretty normal, so there was no need to starting worrying until that point was reached. But… a whole two years? That felt an incredibly long time.

My cousin was a wonderful nanny who helped to look after triplets and twins. Being around children all the time, the tug to have her own children pulled heavy on her heart. When she found her husband-to-be and they later married, they both wanted children straight away, and when it didn't happen for them, every month felt like a year. Thankfully, they now have their own twins through IVF, and their journey was relatively quick on the waiting scale. Another friend of mine, who I would meet up with and talk about this, found the wait very hard because everywhere she turned friends and family were starting to have their own children. Conversations would constantly revolve around nappies, night feeds and all of the beautiful things she wanted to be doing but couldn't. My sister and her husband waited over 10 years in total, and of course the Bible tells of couples who waited almost a lifetime (like Sarah and Abraham).

Waiting is agonising when we have no idea how long it will go on or even if we'll ever reach our goal and the result of this is an emotional pain that is very real. In every situation, if a person is suffering pain due to their circumstances, they are suffering period, and it's important to acknowledge it. Our response should be to come alongside those people – not to suggest solutions or give them pat answers, but simply to show them they are not alone. If they are stuck in self-pity and need to be helped out of that, that's another subject, but real pain and suffering needs real community to come alongside it; to carry and love people back to full health. I know Lindz and I could not have weathered the storm without the amazing people we had around us at the time. There were so many times when we felt our lives were standing still, while everything and everyone else moved on. The support and acknowledgement of friends really helped to combat that feeling.

As we waited, we read so much information it was coming out of our ears. What could be happening? All kinds of issues were cited as possible causes: a low sperm count; one or both parties having some kind of "mechanical" problem; us just not being compatible in one of numerous different ways. Apparently, there were so many things that could go wrong during the small window of time a woman is able to conceive each month, it's a wonder anyone ever gets pregnant! All the more reason to realise that every child is a tiny, perfect little miracle.

The next step was for us to get tested, but this suddenly made it feel so official. We went from the couple "trying" for a baby to the couple with "possible fertility issues", and "potentially unable to conceive naturally, if at all". The words "infertile" and even "barren" started to float around my head, and brought with them new insecurities I hadn't felt before. Surely, the call of every woman is to give birth? We fall in love and we have children, isn't that how the fairy tale goes? Our happy-ever-afters? The thought that I was different scared me and I was beginning to think different just wasn't good enough.

Over the months that followed I was endlessly prodded and poked. One time I fainted but was soon hurried out because they needed the bed. I became a master at hiding yet another cotton swab stuck over the tiny pin prick where they'd taken yet more blood from me. The trips to and from hospital started to mount up and we became dab hands at finding the best parking space and knowing how much money to put in the meter. People often talk of feeling like a human pin cushion when going through these tests, and I started to identify with that description.

Once, I was having a routine internal scan, and when the lady doing the testing finished and cleaned up, she very sweetly announced that she knew who we were and that she loved the band's music. She also mentioned that my brother worked with her husband. At the time my reply was controlled and polite, but it wasn't the best time to be recognised! At the same time, Lindz was having his own human pin cushion experience. He even had an intrusive operation to help his little swimmers, well, swim. He ate so many different vitamin tablets that promised us the world, and the poor guy even had to give up coffee, hot baths and a certain style of underpants to give us more of a winning chance (the things you read on the internet!) We often said out loud, and with incredible faith, that we believed this would all be worth it; that very soon we would hear the right answers. It was just a matter of tweaking how we were doing things and we would get the test results we wanted, so we could move on to the incubating a child bit.

Before long, we did start receiving answers, but they weren't quite the answers we wanted. It is said that approximately 20-30% of couples experiencing infertility receive a diagnosis of "unexplained infertility". Some may view this as a positive thing. In other words, "At least there is nothing more serious we are suffering with…" However, for others, this just brings even more frustration and desperation. How do we know what hurdles we need to jump over next if our predicament is simply unexplained? Looking back, I can see from my journals at the time that I chose to declare hope over our situation, and I have since discovered that hope and pain travel a very close road together.

Diary entry, Friday June 30th, 2006

"We have found out that ours is an 'unexplained infertility', meaning there is no reason we shouldn't be getting pregnant. They have recommended IVF, which should have filled us with fear, questions and disappointment, but as we prayed, I felt protected by a rush of faith which helped me to say out loud, 'God, we will keep praising you, however hard this gets. We will persevere and we WILL trust you.' Any more suffering we walk through as a result of this must, and will, bring more of a determination in us to stay near to God and keep our joy. When I think of the different scenarios we could be going through right now, instead of this, I can't help but feel relief and thank God."

Then, another year went by. WHERE WERE OUR BABIES?!

Slightly reluctantly, we began to talk together about going forward with IVF. IVF stands for "in vitro fertilisation". It means that doctors intervene to fertilise the eggs outside of the woman, then place 1-2 fertilised eggs back into the womb in the hope that they will survive. It is the God-inspired helping hand of science that more and more people need to become pregnant these days, as so many factors are making it harder to conceive quickly, if at all. I am convinced from all the reading I have done that the increased use of birth control medication means a higher percentage of trace elements in our water system, which finds its way into the food we eat, and this likely plays a role in the fact that women's egg production is slowing and they are waiting longer to have children.

Women are born with every single one of their eggs already stored away safely. Over the years, these eggs are released month by month and expelled if they don't fertilise and become a precious child. Once this store has been depleted, there is nothing a woman can do to grow more. This mitigates the chances of conception when so many are waiting for so long to conceive. I totally understand the argument that every woman has the right to forge a career before starting a family – and these days men share the responsibility of childcare more than ever before – but I don't think people realise that if they wait too long, they could be making the choice between having a career or having children, and it can be heart breaking to suddenly realise they've left it too late.

How did we feel about IVF as a couple? Would we be able to cope emotionally? Would this approach fit in with our busy schedules, as we were both frequently on stage and often working 12-hour days? Did we want to be that couple with the big secret hanging over us? We both knew people who would struggle with the thought of us using science to conceive, as opposed to letting it happen naturally. Would those people continue to support us on our journey?

We decided we should at least look into it and see what the professionals had to say. We had nothing to lose by educating ourselves. We did have a few conversations in which we were challenged to think again about using science in this way. We were also given advice such as, "We never used contraception and asked God to keep us from getting pregnant until the time was right." This is amazing, and all the other stories we heard or read about were amazing too, but we had to remember: these were not our story. When we are trying to help people, it's good to remember that for those walking through any kind of challenge or grief, it will NEVER be 100% the same as ours, so we must remain open and not try to fix them or give advice. Love, kindness and a listening ear is most important.

The days passed incredibly slowly, with each month becoming more and more emotionally painful as the signs clearly showed I wasn't pregnant. Yet, while we were moving forward with IVF, educating ourselves about the various paths we could take, this suddenly became our journey, our new hope. Surely soon we'd have our baby? This feeling continued as we walked into our first IVF information meeting. We were greeted by a sea of faces. People were taking their coats off, settling in for the talk; others were taking out notepads; some were looking forlorn and being hugged by their partner, while others looked hopeful and chatted animatedly. Everyone was nervous and we could feel the tension in the room. We were all there for the same reason: we were desperate to be told when we were going to have a child and who was going to help us. No one was really interested in the rest of it – all the details that were explained in that long, laborious meeting – we all just wanted to know how quickly these doctors could put us out of our misery and give us a baby. But this was just the start of a long and complex journey.

Chapter Two

Today me will live in the moment,
Unless it's unpleasant in which case me will eat cookie!
–Cookie Monster

Sitting in that meeting, surrounded by strangers, knowing that each one would now understand us more than our closest friends, I thought about the fact that our long, painful journey waiting to conceive had become an incredibly private, lonely struggle.

We just weren't connecting with people in the same way anymore. We'd hear friends announce that they were pregnant and the reaction from those around them would range from, "Well done mate, you're a real man now!" to a pat on the back and being told they had "super sperm"! Of course, these are hilarious statements when you're the ones celebrating something so life-changing and exciting, but for the couple who are going through the agony of month after month of bad news and broken hearts, it's all too much.

Every time I heard the words "we're pregnant!" my head would swim. What would people say to the expectant couple now? Would any attention be directed towards us? How would my wonderful husband feel when they started reeling out the one-liners to the father-to-be? And the most common thought? Please, God, don't let anyone ask us the dreaded question: "Have you guys thought about having children yet?"

"Umm, let me think… I have thought about nothing else and it's making me want to hyperventilate and run out of the room!"

It became increasingly hard to be among groups of friends. There were brief moments of respite when I could chat to a friend about mundane things – things that helped divert my attention away from the nagging pain inside – but hours before we were due to go out and meet up with people, I would feel anxious. I became nervous about being out in public around groups of people in case the subject of children came up, or a child walked into my field of view and my heart missed a beat. A familiar mix of joy and searing pain rising up inside meant I had to concentrate to keep calm. When I hit my deepest lows, that concentration became a battle inside of me – to smile and say that everything was okay, even if my eyes betrayed my true feelings. Over time, this attitude became my armour, a wall I built around me, and as time went on, I became more adept at hiding behind it. No one apart from a handful of trusted friends were allowed to see behind it.

In her incredible book, Saying Goodbye, (about the grief and challenges of losing a baby) Zoe Clark-Coates writes about having a glass wall between her and the rest of the world. Her words resonated with me so powerfully as I read them:

"For some, this wall [that grief builds] is made of bricks, and they cannot even see the outside world anymore, for others it is glass. My wall was always glass. I could still watch what others were doing, but I was separate from them. On one side of the wall time moved at a normal pace, and on my side things moved slowly. I constantly questioned how life for everyone could just carry on as if nothing had happened, when on my side of the wall, a bomb had been detonated and my world lay in tatters."[1]

The way we interacted with our closest friends slowly became one of the hardest, if not the hardest part of the journey. We are people who love having community around us: family plus friends who feel like family. But as friends of a similar age to us fell pregnant, one by one,

---

1. Zoe Clark-Coates MBE, *Saying Goodbye* (David C. Cook, 2017), pp25-26.

it became harder and harder for us to be around them, which was a bit of a shocker. Of course, they had wonderful news and we wanted to be able to celebrate with them, but it was just so difficult to do so while in the midst of our darkest times. It was especially hard when we overhead friends laughing together about their "mistake" of getting pregnant and wondering aloud what on earth they were going to do now.

Our best friends at that time came to tell us that they were going to start trying for a baby. They wanted to share that information with us, right from the start, as they knew what we were going through. I appreciated this and thought they had given us a good while to prepare, but only a few short weeks later they announced they were pregnant and had scans and celebrations lined up. Plans for the baby's nursery and dreams of snuggles, cooing, and friends visiting naturally filled their thoughts. We knew that it was hard for them to share that news with us, and we really didn't want to be those people who couldn't celebrates someone else's good news, but the truth is, it was REALLY hard to hear, and lots of tears fell.

Close friendships bring real honesty and should be a place where you can let your guard down, so I did. Gemma and I cried together for my brokenness and hugged as we celebrated the incredible news that their lives were going to change forever in a wonderful way. But even that close friendship was harder to maintain after our beautiful god-daughter Eve arrived. It became far easier for me in particular to hide away more and more, and only socialise with people without children, or who had children who were older. I remember a close friend who had suffered a series of miscarriages saying that she became an incredible interior designer in the months that followed, changing her home furnishings over and over again to take her mind off the searing pain she was walking through. I personally became incredibly good at editing photographs and using Photoshop, which incidentally birthed my photography business, Lucy West Images.

Life at this point became very different, very isolated, and I realised I had come face to face with depression. I recognised that a part of me was slowly slipping away. The sweet, carefree, happy girl who only ever saw silver-lined clouds and was much more comfortable with laughter and silliness, was starting to hurt in ways she never thought possible. The pain that threatened to spoil every trip out was immense. Some days it was controllable, but on many others all I could do was slump to the floor crying and rocking before I had the strength to get dressed. I remember perfecting the art of silent screaming as I walked through a shopping mall or found myself in a shop surrounded by beautiful children. I'd rush back to my car shaking, overwhelmed by the noise in my head, but desperately trying to keep my grief a secret.

On those days nothing would remove the pain; nothing would ease it. I was empty, grieving for a child who didn't yet exist but who was wanted with every fibre of my being. Beside my bed, the space between the bed frame and the wall became a familiar spot. I was squashed in, hidden there, but I felt safe. It was a safe place to collapse and let out those deep cries, without having to explain why, without having to reveal what was going on inside my broken little heart. I cried until my head hurt, my eyes were swollen, and my throat burned, but it was a release – a letting go of all that I couldn't put into words. How long could this go on for? Surely, we had already done our time? We'd already had a couple of years of deep pain, which by now felt like a lifetime.

Since coming through the heavy fog of pain, I have learned more and more about the isolation one can feel in these situations; the feeling we can carry that we are utterly alone in our suffering. We may not be physically "alone" yet find it impossible to share our grief with the people we are closest to, who simply won't understand it on an emotional level.

I have also learned that it's okay that people don't understand. Yes, it's painful when people say or do silly things, but the truth is, we only truly understand something when we have walked a similar road ourselves. We can't get angry at others for not knowing what something feels like.

As more couples in our social sphere became pregnant, conversations naturally turned to that event, looking forward with excitement and hope as plans were made. Then, when the baby, arrived, their lives were changed as this little person took up every moment of the new parents' time. Unsurprisingly, the new arrival was the most important and incredible thing in their lives. But when you are in pain, you can't cope with conversations about children on a regular basis; questions about playgroup here, a chat about nappies there. If you're feeling really strong, then maybe you could just about make it through a baby shower before racing home to cry.

Yet, me choosing to spend so much time alone was making our problem a whole lot worse. At the time I wasn't fully aware of why it was making things worse. To me, it felt like withdrawing was a good solution, instead of having to hear and see things that broke my heart. But after listening to a TED talk by Brené Brown, I suddenly had an epiphany. She is an incredible researcher and puts into words the science behind community and connection with others. The words she uses are so simple yet so profound, summarising and describing the deepest of human needs – to connect with those around us. I would thoroughly recommend a listen to her findings!

This and other studies say that our brains are wired for connection; that we need connection to give purpose and meaning to our lives. Without such connection we can quite easily fall into feelings of shame, of not feeling good enough around people who seem to be doing better than us, or who have the things we want. This is how I was starting to feel. Would others accept me if they saw the reality of my situation and understood that I was incapable of producing the one thing that half the population seemed able to do easily? And yet, to be "seen" we must make ourselves vulnerable, which means putting aside the shame and choosing not to worry about what people will think of the real me. We also need to show compassion and kindness to ourselves, which takes courage – the courage to be imperfect. However, the circle had begun to form around me. I was avoiding connection because it hurt, even though connection was precisely what I needed, and all the time I was in hiding, I couldn't be seen or understood. I wasn't being fully loved and wasn't able to fully love others (something that had always brought my life colour and joy). In short, my life was losing its meaning and purpose.

If we choose to believe that, even though we are imperfect and mess up, we are worthy of being loved, worthy of belonging somewhere, that our vulnerability and flaws are beautiful and not something to hide away… well, that's it. Bit by bit we can become what we believe, living day-to-day far more confidently than before. Conversely, all the time we think we're not good enough, we will more than likely see this reflected in our speech and actions. Unaware of what we are projecting to others, this can help to push people away. Without us realising it, we are helping to fuel the lie that we really aren't good enough. Breaking this circle takes courage. We need to believe that we are worthy, and declare it out loud. Our journey need not define who we are. Whatever difficulties and pain we have faced, they merely describe a state we were in at one moment in time, not WHO we are. It is so good to declare out loud the truth that we are chosen and accepted, and to kick those negative and often self-pitying attitudes to the floor.

That's easy to write but, of course, can be hard to do.

When I realised how I was closing myself in, cutting myself off, I was acutely aware that breaking the circle was going to be far more difficult than it sounded. First, I had to pick myself up off the floor before I could think about declaring anything positive over myself! Guilt says, "Sorry, I made a mistake" but shame says, "Sorry, I am a mistake". Shame was the major factor that prevented me from connecting with others, especially those who had become mothers.

The media plays its part in perpetrating shame and so often we believe the lies it feeds us. Women: we must be the best mum and wife, cook healthy, delicious meals, look stylish and be well groomed, be slim, healthy, strong, full of energy and, of course, be a successful businesswoman on the side! Men: you mustn't be weak, you must show you have it all together; you've got to have the car, the gym membership, the watch, the right aftershave, a beautiful lady by your side and the golf clubs. When these things don't materialise, or we feel we are failing compared to our peers, shame can creep in, which can lead to us hiding our true selves from others. We put on a good show, or we simply remove ourselves from friends, even family members – anyone who makes the shame feel worse – resulting in upset and confusion for them and loneliness for us.

The root of feeling unworthy is the fear of not fitting in. As children growing up, it's one of the biggest fears we carry. Not being picked for the team, left standing alone in the playground, not having someone to hold hands with on the school trip… Lindz and I were now confronting this fear as adults, feeling like we no longer fit in. We often talked together about where we belonged. Who were our real friends? Did people want to be around us? Had we suddenly become outcasts – the ones who needed "fixing"? Was it hard work to hang out with us because we were damaged goods? Did people with children worry about inviting us out, in case they put their foot in it and reminded us we weren't part of the elusive "parenting club" that so many talked about? (a feeling I'm sure was compounded by Mothercare, with their series of adverts ending in #welcometotheclub – a phrase that always had me running for the tissues). We found ourselves socialising more often with parents of older children, which felt far more comfortable, and it was actually lovely to learn lots of parenting tips just by watching how they did it!

This season was a time of immense learning too. Lindz and I were learning who we were as a married couple living with deep disappointment. We were learning how to cope with the pain together not just alone, and learning how to be truly positive and celebrate others, not just put on a brave face and get through it. I have heard it said on several occasions, and I wholly agree, that you will never truly appreciate something you have until you are able to celebrate when others receive it before you. Jealousy can break a person in two and I didn't want it to steal another moment from me. But this was a hard process, especially when we heard about couples having unplanned pregnancies that were described as a "mistake" or an "inconvenience", or that the resulting child was "hard work … difficult … robbing us of our social life". Pain struck me again and again as I read daily comments from mothers about their children on Facebook. I felt angry at the many off-hand comments and wanted to shout, Why the heck did you have children if you don't even want them around or treasure the time you have with them?!

* * *

After the initial meeting described at the beginning of this chapter, it took a few months of waiting before we finally received a phone call inviting us to visit St Mary's Hospital for a consultation, but it wasn't incredible news. The person on the phone said it was, "So we can assess whether you are eligible to go on the waiting list for IVF." Rather than an answer this was another question mark. A consultation to see if we could be added to another waiting list?! How long was all this going to take for goodness sake?

In due course, we met with a doctor who had a huge black moustache and a bit of a lisp, and heard from him that we would have to wait another 18 months before beginning the process, which would in itself take several months. Yes, we were facing two… more… years. I left the doctor's office feeling very low, while my lovely, positive husband saw it as the next step on the ladder rather than another long wait.

We were both in different bands when we began looking into infertility treatment. Lindz was in LZ7 and I was still in BlushUK. We both travelled a lot and wondered how we would be able to juggle IVF treatment with our rather crazy schedules. This led me to have a very tearful and honest conversation with a wonderful older, wiser friend of mine, Sue. She asked me some deeply difficult questions, which I was so grateful for, and I cried my way through them to find the answers I was dreading but knew deep down. After a while, a very sad conclusion was reached: I would need to leave the band if I was to have any hope of continuing with IVF and my dream of having a family. My whole world was about to change … again.

For years I had described myself as a singer. It is still one of my deepest passions. I sang for years in different bands and on very different sized stages, from church halls in front of tiny youth groups to more than 170,000 people in Dallas, Texas. I sang to tens of thousands of people in live audiences, via television screens, and in many schools over the years. I literally didn't think I could do anything else. After my time with the band V*enna finished, I felt so broken, but BlushUK had brought me real joy again. I had started and then grown this band. It was my work baby, the thing that defined me, gave me purpose and got me out of bed every morning. But I realised that if I wanted children, I needed to walk away from it all and start again. We had just recorded an EP which I'd had quite a big hand in writing, yet I'd have to give up this too, before it had been properly toured and marketed. I felt the pressure not only of letting the girls down, but also our record company. They had sown a lot into us and really believed in us. I also felt personally cheated in many ways, as I wanted to be the one touring our new songs, not a new set of girls.

It felt crushing having to tell people my decision. The girls in BlushUK were brilliant when I told them the news. We cried together, talked, laughed and shared some of our fears and joys concerning the changes. After that, our day-to-day routine stayed pretty much the same for a few months, then by Christmas 2007 I was done. Seven years at The Message Trust were over. It had been my safe place, helping me fulfil many dreams at the same time as growing as a person in lots of different ways. At my final Message Christmas prayer day, my boss and friend Andy Hawthorne dressed up as Santa and sang to me, I'll have a blue, blue Christmas, without you. I cried happy tears on and off for most of the afternoon and didn't think about how embarrassed I would be when I watched back the videos of me giving my, "Goodbye everyone, I love you all so much!" speech. They were my family, and I was going to miss them all terribly!

January 2008 was spent staring vacantly at a computer screen with tears in my eyes. Leaving V*enna had been a similar experience. Our American record company had wanted us to move to the US and pour ourselves into making the band very successful, and I'm sure we could have done that if Lindz and I had not been about to step into the huge but beautiful commitment of marriage. Lindz felt it was right to continue his work in the UK, so I had a big decision to make. I know long-distance relationships can stretch you, but this was a step too far, so I decided to step down and follow my husband-to-be.

After leaving BlushUK, a funny twist of circumstances birthed a new career. I had a whole month waiting for my CRB check to come through, so that I could do some supply teaching, and in the meantime, I edited the images of my cousin's beach wedding, which she had asked me to photograph on New Year's Eve. I got into Photoshop, read tutorials online, practiced, and edited over and over again until I knew the software like the back of my hand. And there, without planning to, I began my next career as a freelance photographer. I'd always loved photography, so why not? The plan seemed to open up seamlessly before me. I could fit in the IVF treatment as well as a bit of supply teaching, and bring in enough money to keep us going. It sounded perfect… if only I could just forget who I was and how I felt when I was singing, that is. These were hard times, but by the grace of God I managed to keep a glimmer of hope and excitement about the ever-looming IVF.

Lindz was brilliant throughout the process. We had many low or hard moments, as you might expect, but on the whole, he really looked after me and stayed incredibly positive, even though he could have been crying inside. I just couldn't have done it without him and will always be grateful that he didn't just give up on me and look for an easy way out. It is quite normal for women to worry, at some point on this journey, that their husbands or partners will leave them to find someone else who can give them the children they so desire. But even though I let those thoughts cross my mind on a number of occasions, I knew deep down that, thank goodness, Lindz was in this for the long run.

Sadly, many couples do split under the strain of waiting for children, which I just can't imagine going through on top of everything else. In fact, studies have shown that couples are three times more likely to break up after failed fertility treatment.[2] To lose your soulmate while struggling with infertility must be horrendous, and I am now passionate about making sure that women who confide in me are keen to walk this with their other half, and not alone. The moments when Lindz collapsed became my lowest moments too. To see the person you love so broken is very painful. But, thank goodness, for the majority of the time he literally oozes optimism. He was great at turning our situation around

2. Source: Medical Daily online, https://www.medicaldaily.com)

and seeing that we were just one step closer, not that the carrot being dangled was further away, as my battered heart often felt.

Lindz and I found that choosing not to blame each other – not allowing the thought that there could be some kind of escape route – means that our relationship is rock solid now. We feel so sure that we will love each other and be soulmates for the rest of our lives. It was not always easy to think like this, not easy to talk to one another like we believed it, but it has been more than worth it. I don't take what I've just written for granted when I think back to that time, because men and women see and experience this journey so differently. We are blessed to still be together – I know that. For a woman, the emotional side is deeply intense; for men, the pressure of not being able to give their wife/partner a child can bring immense pressure, like a physical weight. On my side, there were more tears; on Lindz' side, more anger and frustration. Wonderfully, he has written the next chapter in this book to share his insights. Men are often as deeply affected as women, yet don't always get their voices heard. We must let men be honest and open about their struggles and apparent failures, as we know that talking brings incredible release.

Chapter Three

Attitude is the difference between an ordeal and an adventure.
–Unknown

The Weight (by Lindz West – a male perspective)

I was standing in the kitchen of our home in Manchester when Lucy came downstairs and said, "It's happened again Lindz… I don't think it's worked." My heart broke and I felt a physical weight on my shoulders. My posture changed from tall and upright, ready to face the world, to slumped and heavily burdened. I recalled being in a high school in Cornwall on one of our LZ7 tours. I was sitting in the disabled toilet – the only place where I could find some privacy – when I first heard those words. "Lindz, I'm so sorry, it's not worked. I bled a load this morning and I'm gonna have to get myself a hospital check-up." Then the same thing happened again. Boom! Here comes the WEIGHT. The weight of the question why? Why us? Why Lucy and why me? The weight that lies heavily on so many men going through the journey of infertility. It's mostly unseen and rarely spoken about. Instead it's hidden, bottled up.

I remember getting onto the tour bus after a school day in Wigan. We were elated after such a great day of taking lessons, speaking about Jesus, seeing self-harm reversed and suicides aborted, literally in school! We sat in the bus buzzing and, as per usual, had a little back and forth banter about the day. We chatted about what a young person had asked me in class, about the crazy dance moves we'd seen, and about the reaction from the young people and students to the LZ7 stuff. These were the best times – we were tired, yet fulfilled!

But that pumped feeling soon dissipated as Lucy called again. I kind of knew what was coming. This was the day when we would find out if she was pregnant or not. "It's not worked Lindz. This time the eggs didn't even attach or multiply. I'm so sorry." What kind of face was I supposed to hold now? What was I supposed to say to everyone in the bus, as they all went quiet while I spoke to Lucy? Who in the world could I talk to about this deep, guttural wrench that made me want to punch the closest person to me? I didn't punch anyone, of course, instead I did the classic "man" trick of bottling it up, hoping that I could take it out on something later.

I had no one to talk to and felt that no one would understand anyway. I didn't particularly feel shame about the whole situation, I just felt gutted! That's the best way I can describe it. Lucy and I were at a great church in Manchester that was super community focused, and we both served on youth and kids' teams whenever I was in the country. At this point in time we had a good support network around us but (and I write the word "but" very carefully, as I am sure the people at the time meant well) there was little help or understanding for a guy going through this. I didn't know how to share it and process it all, and no one else seemed to know how to deal with what I was going through.

It was around this time that we met the Clarks, Dave and Jo, a family whose youngest son, Isaac, had invited me to go snowboarding for this 10th birthday at the Manchester indoor slope. He was a major LZ7 fan and his kind sister, Harriet, had called and asked if I would get to know him a little bit – be a big brother figure for him. Of course, Lucy and I went along, and while Lucy got to know Jo, I talked to Dave. I shared the story of what was happening, and I clearly remember Dave saying, "Go to Turkey for a break." I was like, "Say that again mate!" The break was incredible, but more importantly this was the start of me being able to share with someone outside of LZ7's gigging, touring, preaching, church world; someone who just wanted to know me for me – nothing else. Dave was an utter legend – the kind of guy you want to be when you grow up. He listened and didn't try to come up with some solution. He just listened. If you are reading this, you need that too, I promise. It will be the saviour of your mental health and wellbeing to allow someone else to endorse you as man and blow away those "half-man half-failure" thoughts that can creep in throughout this process. "You are not that," I kept telling myself.

Lucy and I never dreamt that our family-making plans would face problems. We didn't realise there would be complications until, at the age of 29, we decided it was time to start. We had been married and "practising" for children for four years and just thought, "Now feels like a good time to get the ball rolling and start". The next few months threw up some slight concerns, but when that turned into 18 months, we went to see a doctor.

As a kid growing up, I played every sport under the sun and was no stranger to smelly locker rooms, so I was genuinely not bothered about having a doctor probe about and look into the, let's call them "mechanics", of the baby-making process! The doctors could see that we were both healthy, kept ourselves in good shape, ate healthily, got enough sleep, and so on. From the outside there were no apparent issues. I had to submit a sperm sample at the surgery. My first words, as I handed over the bottle to the practitioner, were, "Is that any good then, mate?" thinking I was the man for being able to get done what many blokes might find a very awkward situation. That was just my way of dealing with it! The coping strategies we employ when under the cosh come straight to the surface, especially when they concern a man's privacy. The age old saying that "men don't talk about money or marriage" dissipates as soon as one is forced to face it. For me, having a solid sense of humour helped me to deal with the doctors and nurses who were looking into all kinds of places. If humour is not your thing, perhaps recording your thoughts in a journal would help. Just get those thoughts out of your head and express them in some way.

Another thing that helped me throughout the process was keeping up a fitness regime and going regularly to the gym. This helped me to focus my mind and channel my pent-up energy into something positive. I've always kept fit, but during the years of infertility, and later through the journey of adoption, this became a real foundation for my life. If you're not into going to the gym, any activity that will help you to focus on something else and transport you away for a while can only be a good thing. I use the play on words "the weight" because this stuff weighs heavily on men, and is something they find hard to share and talk about. Staying fit and having some balance in my life helped me to carry that weight.

The doctors arranged an appointment for Lucy to have her ovaries checked, first by ultrasound then by a probe, which apparently is similar to having a smear test, and I was due to get the results of my sperm sample, so in due course we found ourselves back in the doctor's surgery. The doctor looked at my results, then at me and said, "Mr West, we've had your results back and your 'swimmers' (as he put it) are slightly drunk. They are marathon runners rather than sprinters, so they're not making their way directly to the egg in the way we want them to. Your sperm count is not low, it's just wobbly." In my head I was thinking, Drunk and wobbly? That's hilarious! It was his kind way of putting it and he said that I would have to go to the hospital for a referral.

Like I said, I'm not the reserved type when it comes to examinations, so when the doctor had a feel around the baby-making apparatus and said, "Cough, please" I wasn't at all disturbed – that was until he said, "Hmm…" Okay, what did "hmm" actually mean? He explained that I had a vein growing around my mechanics that was literally choking and heating up my swimmers, which is why they were drunk and wobbly and not sprinting out of the blocks. "To get them to speed up," he informed me, "we're going to have to remove this vein."

Because I had played everything from table tennis to American football, anywhere from county to national level, when I was younger, I'd definitely taken more than my fair share of hits. I remember taking several ill-timed smacks from cricket balls or getting fists and elbows to the mechanics. Aged 11, I needed to have a hernia drained after I had been hit pretty hard in the nether regions and my mum had noticed a certain elephantiasis in that area. My testicles were the size of small melons, and this happened twice! However, it was sorted out at the time and the doctors assured us there would be no ongoing side effects.

So, in due course I found myself booked in for surgery to have this small vein removed under local anaesthetic. Picture this: I'd just come off tour and here I was, wearing a hospital gown, waiting for someone to stick a knife in my privates, and I would be able to watch the whole thing! However, things were about to get more complicated. Because I'd had surgery in this area before, there was scar tissue which made it inaccessible. The surgeon sat me down and said, "Mr West, we are not able to go in at the actual area. We're going to have to thrombose the vein (i.e. cut off the blood supply until it dies) and we're going to go in at your neck."

My NECK?!!

I was dumbfounded. How in the world could that even work?

He patiently explained that the jugular vein that runs down from the brain is actually attached to your mechanics, so he could reach the vein in question by going down through the jugular. "You can do what?!" I said, amazed. Having agreed the way forward, I lay on the operating table and had two lots of anaesthetic: one jab just above my collar bone, and another in the neck muscle a couple of inches below my ear. While we waited for it to take effect, a screen was positioned above my head, so I could watch what was going on.

It was an X-ray screen connected to a camera and I could see my whole insides! I wasn't freaked out by this, just in awe of it all. Once the anaesthetic had kicked in, the surgeon grabbed his scalpel and told me to look away. With my face partially covered with blue paper, he made an incision in my neck, which was accompanied by an audible sploosh sound, a load of blood splashed across my face. The surgeon took what looked like a straw and pushed it into my vein. This was followed by an implement I can only describe as looking like a bike brake cable with a metal spider on the end of it. This sounds pretty freaky now, writing it down, but the doctor calmly talked me through every part of the process. The cable with the spider was a piece of titanium that would be fed down through my body to reach the offending vein. He explained that he would twist the cable to open up the spider, which would form a blockage in the vein to prevent the blood from flowing.

So, it began. Up and down he went, at least twenty times with twenty little titanium spiders. Mid-procedure I had a thought. "I can see the cable going up and down my body on the X-ray screen but why can't I feel anything?" I asked the doctor and he said to me,

"Can you feel the blood going around your body?"

"No," I replied.

"That's because there are no nerves in your veins or arteries," he explained. "You won't feel a thing… though you will later, to be honest."

Thrombosing a vein in a sensitive area like this would give me the sensation of having been punched in the mechanics for a week to ten days, he told me.

Once the procedure was complete, I waited around twenty minutes for the cut to heal, then just walked out of the hospital, ready for the next hoop I would need to jump through. I felt fine, but it hit me a day later. Holy smokes! I've never felt a dull pain like it. The little vein that was causing these issues was starting to die, but it wasn't going to go quietly without a fight! I constantly had that "dead leg" feeling, but at least I knew something good would come from it.

Even though this story sounds traumatic, a positive mindset carried me through it. Rather than thinking, Oh, no, this is an ordeal! I was always looking ahead: if I do this, then this will happen. I focused on the goal rather than the issue in front of me. Though, trust me, every day when I woke up, I had to remind myself that it was all for the greater good.

Why have I told you this story? Because it's all part of the journey. I genuinely had the attitude that such problems would never happen to me. I constantly wondered, "Why is this happening to me? I'm the frontman of a band that speaks to young people about living their life on purpose. I motivate young people, I travel, I preach that I'm this, I'm that..." All this was going on in my head, behind the scenes, but I was hiding it really well – or so I thought.

LZ7 schools' lessons are high energy, full of stories of hope in the face of disaster, coupled with the life-changing message of Jesus. In every lesson, to this day, there is a point in one of the stories where, if I'm on my own, I will just crack and have a cry to myself over the lives of the young people in the class. It's pure passion to see them achieve their full potential in Jesus. But during this time, the tears came from a deep hurt because I was stuck in a situation for which I had no answers. I was going through test after test, and watching Lucy go through even more rigorous tests than me – and as her husband, I felt helpless. I had to talk to someone. At this point I realised that what was needed was for me to just gently listen to Lucy – not offer solutions. No, "What if we did this… or that… or what if we paid for this, or met with this or that doctor?" Instead, this was a time to make sure she felt listened to, even though I was at the bottom of my own pit.

I remember driving through Manchester one day, near to the end of our first IVF session. I felt a lightness – you know, that feeling when finally, you become debt free, or your fave tune comes on the radio and you're overwhelmed with that Friday feeling. Yeah, that! It felt as though life had suddenly completed itself and all was good with the world. In fact, we were both super excited as we sat, with incredible anticipation, in the waiting room of a private clinic embarking on a course of IVF treatment that looked like it was going to work. We had jumped through all the hoops (well, let's be honest, Lucy had), been through the daily injections, the visits to the hospital to check the progress of the treatment, and the daily logging of all our emotions.

One of the funniest moments in all of this was when Lucy was having an examination and I was sat outside the room. The doctor was having a look around Lucy's baby making parts when she suddenly raised her head and said, "I will keep praying for you guys. I know who Lindz is and I'll keep you in my prayers." When the check was done, Lucy literally leapt off the bed, legged it out of the examination room and grabbed me. "She knows us!" she gasped as we hastily exited the hospital. Looking back, I can see how all this was such a secret for us, and it brought with it the kind of shame that lay just beneath the surface. The fact that the doctor knew us made us want to bolt, and we couldn't get out of there quickly enough!

Alongside the moments of hope were many tough days. While all this was going on, I was still front facing at festivals, tours and schools; literally holding it together with bravest face I could muster. I even wrote a song called Brave Face to try and express some of the underlying emotion that was going on under the skin. I'm a solution guy, to be honest. I always try to find creative ways to make things happen. You could call me a bit of Del boy! "Next year Rodders, we'll be mwillionaires" has always been my attitude to life. So, to be faced with the prospect of not being able to "make it happen" was a daily kick in the teeth.

Over the years I had seen statements like, "It's not what happens to you that counts, it's how you deal with it". In fact, I'd seen a million similar resilience quotes, and none of them had made me feel any better. These feelings were amplified all the more by all my mates having babies. That's one of the most difficult things to face as a bloke. It's a gut-wrenching feeling when you're happy for a mate and his family, but the smile masks a deep desire for that to be you one day. The secret is, it will be you. Whether you become a dad physically, spiritually, through adoption, or by becoming a stepdad, being a dad can take many guises. You may be stuck on the idea that the conventional route to fatherhood is the only route, but in reality, there are many.

I know that many people will have experienced similar feelings. The emotions are tough to deal with but there is absolutely no shame in infertility. Nor any shame in the adoption process we later decided to pursue. Many men want to know that God's plan for their lives is Plan A. Blokes have an innate part of us that wants to be in control of everything, but that means we are susceptible to feel like we are spinning out of control when there seems to be no hope of moving forward. As Lucy has explained, we are both Churchies, and our faith in Jesus has been our foundation, the bedrock to everything we've experienced. I fully believe that people are not accidents; their lives are ordained and designed. Some enter this world through the "homegrown" route and some through the "chosen" route. Whichever way they arrive, that route is still God's PLAN A!

My faith has played a huge part in this process and understanding who I am in God as a bloke has been vital for me. Ephesians 1:4-14 in The Message says this:

"Long before he laid down earth's foundations, he had us in mind, had settled on us as the focus of his love, to be made whole and holy by his love. Long, long ago he decided to adopt us into his family through Jesus Christ. (What pleasure he took in planning this!) He wanted us to enter into the celebration of his lavish gift-giving by the hand of his beloved Son."

That describes us. That's you and me. Wherever you find yourself today on the journey of infertility – whether in hope or in the depths of the darkest moment – know that you are a unique person who has been adopted into God's huge, wider family. He says that you are His – His son, His daughter. He lavishes His love on you, even when you don't notice it. He looks for you and says, "You are mine." Whatever happens on your journey, whether fertile or infertile, God's Plan A for your life is incredible. I hope you manage to walk into all that He has for you. And remember, talk, talk, talk. Find that place where you can express your anxieties and, in all things, keep God close.

I am now Dad to two beautiful little "chosen" humans. They are the answer to the promise I received that one day I would be a dad. The method of making this family was not the one I thought we would have to go through. Would I change that? Absolutely not! I remember the point at which I realised, "Kids don't define me as a dad, or a man. God defines me as a son with a perfect plan". That was the moment the WEIGHT lifted off me. I finally understood that I didn't need to strive to become something that perhaps God had not determined me to be. The weight of all that pressure can break a man, but Jesus said, "My yoke is easy and my burden is light" (Matthew 11:30). Stick close to Jesus. If you're reading this and you don't know Him yet, get to know Him. Trust me, the burden, the weight, the responsibility, is picked up, shared and halved when Jesus is in the picture. This journey doesn't make us weak, incomplete versions of ourselves, it just challenges us to lean further into Jesus; to listen before searching for a solution; to find our identity in whose we are rather than who we are.

Whether you go the "chosen" route or the "homegrown" route, remember the plan that God has for you is PLAN A. There is no Plan B.

The Weight (written by Lucy – a female perspective)

I really wanted Lindz to include some of what he went through on this journey, as so often the focus is on how the woman feels and what she is experiencing. It can be easy to bypass men and forget about their deep emotions.

Statistics tell us that the highest rates of suicide recorded are among men aged 40-45[3] and that these rates are three times higher than the comparable rates for women. Studies don't often cite fertility problems as a specific reason for suicide, but professionals say that speaking to someone can dramatically reduce suicidal thoughts and feelings, and men can often be left behind when they're hurting – the assumption being that they can just "have a beer and get over it".

If someone is going through something this difficult and seems to be considering suicide, encourage them to talk about how they are feeling. Listening is the best way to help. Avoid offering solutions or making judgements, and encourage them to seek professional help from someone who knows how to get to the root of the problem and show them that hope is there.

---

3. https://www.nhs.uk/news/mental-health/uks-suicide-rate-highest-among-middle-aged-men/

On the whole, men often find it harder to express their feelings. Fertility does not equate to manhood (or womanhood) as some people make out, but I'm sure that a man's sense of self can be damaged when they think along these lines and hear those offhand comments like, "Well done mate, super sperm, you're a real man now" etc.

When men find it hard to discuss deep things and their emotional impact, that's when the wait becomes the weight – a heavy burden that is never addressed. Although challenging, a man needs to find the right outlet to talk about this with people he trusts. Maybe with family and friends, on a boys' weekend away, or perhaps with a counsellor. Some men find it helpful to be part of an online support group, whether for men only or mixed, where they can talk openly about their feelings and share their problems anonymously.

Men can often feel that they are letting their partner down, even though it is a medical problem and out of their control. Some can be incredibly embarrassed about it and experience feelings of shame, which prevents them from revealing it to other male friends. Of course, infertility is no one's "fault" but the psychological hurdle can be a hard one to get over.

The emotional burden falls harder on men than society at large might expect. Difficulty conceiving and a diagnosis of infertility is stressful and upsetting. Although discussions around infertility frequently focus on women, men can carry feelings of shame, anger, grief, helplessness and frustration. This can be compounded by the feeling that they have to suppress their emotions in order to remain supportive of their partner.

A helpful thing to remember is that so much about infertility is not absolute, and there are things a man can do to improve the situation. When men are told that they can do certain things to help, this helps them to feel more in control – and when anyone feels in control, they are less stressed and more able to cope. Men's emotions have been closely linked to action. In other words, they need to find ways to "do something" or "find a solution". Sitting down to talk about and share their emotions may seem to some men to detract from taking action, whereas women are more comfortable stopping to talk about the issues they are facing. There were times when Lindz felt he wasn't "man enough" because he couldn't get the job done in the natural way. It was so hard to see him going through that.

Men and women, while equal in so many ways, are still very far apart. Not only is our physiology different but we have been socialised differently too. From a physiological standpoint, people generally consider that men don't carry such strong emotions as women, yet research shows that men's immune and cardiovascular systems take longer to recover when they experience extreme emotion – more so than women's. Scientists say that men experience more negative health issues when faced with severe emotions than women. Since discussing emotions is not hard-wired into men the way it is with women, this can be a reason why healing does not come as quickly.

Chapter Four

My grace is sufficient for you, for my power is made perfect in your weakness.
2 Corinthians 12:9

Months had turned into years and we still didn't have our promise, but we were not just sitting still and waiting, we were bravely moving towards it. When we did our first round of IVF, it was actually very exciting. I was getting looked after and was praised for being brave by the few close friends who knew. I would get lots of cuddles from Lindz and my mum when they saw the bruising from the injections, and I got to relax a LOT during that time (something I loved and rarely got to do because life was always so hectic). I remember my friend, who has diabetes, and I going into the toilet at a pub during a birthday celebration, where we both injected together while giggling about how this would look to others if they saw us! I was so full of hope and excitement, fully believing my time was coming. I can see why people are happy to continue doing IVF over and over; that feeling can be quite addictive.

Practically speaking, the process is pretty straight forward; what goes on inside the body is far more intricate. First, I had to take medication to suppress my natural menstrual cycle. This makes the medicines used in the next stage far more effective. This stage lasted about two weeks. Then I changed to another medication, FSH (Follicle Stimulating Hormone), which I injected for about 10-12 days, and which stimulated my ovaries to increase the amount of eggs I produced. Finally, there was a single injection of HCG (Human Chorionic Gonadotropin) before going in for surgery.

I was given a huge package full of little tiny bottles, which rattled about, making a beautiful symphony of clinks and clonks. Then there was an ominous-looking recycling bin for those bottles, and the needles and syringes used to administer the medication. I had to mix the correct medicines together, using a new needle each time to draw out the liquid and inject it into my tummy. Sometimes I would hit a little vein and it would cause ugly bruising – my precious war wounds. The first few times I did it, I remember getting through my, "5… 4… 3… 2… 1… GO!" countdown several times before I finally stuck the needle in. But, other than a pin prick, there was minimal pain, so this wasn't an issue for someone who isn't too bothered about needles.

To make sure the risk of OHSS (Ovarian Hyperstimulation Syndrome) was minimised (meaning to avoid producing too many eggs at once) I needed to attend hospital regularly to have an ultrasound or blood test, so the doctors could check how I was doing all the way through. This process showed them (and us) how many follicles were growing inside my ovaries. They would check the strength and maturity of each one to work out how many eggs they'd be able to harvest when the time was right. When the nurses felt that my eggs were almost ready, I had to go in daily to be monitored, which was very time consuming as the clinic was a 20-minute drive away in good traffic. The penultimate part of the process was to receive the HCG injection – a hormone produced by the placenta after implantation, in order to feed the egg that becomes attached to the uterine wall. This was administered about 36 hours before I would have those precious eggs removed. The hormone injection can also trigger the natural process of ovulation, which sends the eggs to a place where they can be retrieved by doctors from the ovaries. This last injection was essential, and I remember feeling ever so nervous about getting the timing just right and not messing up the whole treatment, especially as the operation to remove the eggs was already scheduled for 36 hours later.

Once the daily injections and hospital visits were done, and the final hormones were in, then it was a waiting game. I felt so emotional during those final one and a half days. Maybe it was the hormones, or maybe it was because we were so close to the end. The reality of what we were doing weighed heavy on my heart, yet at the same time I was expectant, waiting patiently for something truly wonderful. I did believe at the time that we would be one of the success stories. I believed I would be among the 40% or so of women my age who conceive through IVF, with no problems at all. I was fit and healthy. This was going to happen for sure.

With the agonising 36-hour wait over, finally it was time for my egg removal. We went to the hospital and I was wheeled to the operating theatre. I was anaesthetised and said the obligatory crazy stuff as I went under. While under sedation, a fine needle was passed into my ovaries and the eggs were pulled out. These were then passed onto the embryology team for checking. What a miracle in the making! I do wonder how on earth doctors manage these intricate operations. They really are true heroes every day of their lives.

I found myself waking up and drifting off into a dreamless, heavy sleep, over and over again for a couple of hours, while my beautiful husband patiently sat by my bedside waiting and smiling at me every time I groggily came around. I smiled back at him then nodded off again. The highlight of being in hospital for me was the staff bringing the food round: macaroni cheese with mustard in the cheese sauce, absolutely delicious! I can still taste it now as I write. I'm sure it wasn't healthy in the slightest, but it tasted SO good! The guy who brought it round let me take the whole tray home and I was eating my favourite comfort food for ages as I recovered. It was a small thing, but I was so grateful. A few hours later I was home and resting again. I'd never done so much sitting around; what a luxury!

We waited for a few long, question-filled days, then returned to have the fertilised eggs put back into my womb. Would we have any strong ones? How many would they put back in? The doctors told us that we had two big, strong, healthy fertilised eggs that had been grown in tiny little incubators, and were now ready to go back into their mummy, hopefully for 9 months of growing before we met them again. Wow! We saw them on the screen: twins, "big, strong and healthy" in the words of the doctor. Our two little fighters with a great chance of living and bringing us so much joy. It was a strange feeling, as if we were actually meeting our babies for the first time and connecting with them. I know some people believe that a baby is not a human with rights until they are born, which is why abortion can be explained away so easily. There is a quote by an unknown author which says,

"If scientists find one single cell on Mars, they are willing to declare there is life on Mars, but they see a baby forming inside a womb and they are unwilling to call it life."

I like and dislike this quote in equal measure, because it honours and disregards life in the same sentence. I understand that not every scientist shares this view, but it is making a point about honouring life from the very start. There are many differing beliefs out there, and everyone has their reasons for believing what they do, but the Bible teaches that we are all precious to God even before we are conceived. This truth has shaped my thoughts to believe that all life (and with it, the possibility of a wonderful future) begins as soon as those little eggs fertilise.

So, there they were: our babies! So many possibilities. If they lived, there was so much life, hope and future contained in those tiny eggs. If they died, we were back to square one; back to our uphill struggle. But we were even more determined after seeing them on the screen. We said a prayer over our little ones and after a couple of minutes they were back in. The beginning of another journey.

Much of the next 17 days were spent in my dressing gown as I worried that any lifting or heavy movements would dislodge the eggs and I would lose them. These were our babies and they were SO wanted and longed for. I knew that if they didn't make it, I was going to mourn them as if they'd been kicking inside me. After a few days, I went back to work part time as a supply teacher in the school around the corner from home. A few teachers knew and wouldn't let me do any lifting, which was sweet, so it was quite a lovely time even though we were facing so many uncertainties. Would this work? What if they both took and we had twins?! How would my body respond to pregnancy? What would our lives be like if it did work? What if we lost them? Could we afford to do IVF again? Would they have any disabilities due to our age? How would we tell our family and friends? What if we fell in love with these growing babies then lost them later in the pregnancy, or worse, when we'd met them and fallen in love with them? What would their personalities be like? Would they look more like Lindz or me? Hopefully they would get my eyes and Lindz's incredible legs! There were so many questions about the coming months and years, questions that I'm sure every parent ponders, even if they conceive naturally.

Finally, the wait was over. It was day 17 – a Sunday. The day we were due to take the pregnancy test, though I already knew in my heart what the result would be. I had bled heavily in the shower the day before, more than I was used to, and it had made me cry. I had heard that a bit of bleeding during pregnancy is perfectly normal, but this was more than just a little and didn't feel very normal at all. Yet at times I was resolute, despite the bleeding.

If my God can do miracles, then why not now with our babies? If the timing is right, then these babies will be alive and growing well!

I did the pregnancy test, then Lindz and I busied ourselves like there was nothing going on, almost to deny that it was really happening. I felt a sense of guilt, that somehow it was my fault that we'd lost our precious babies, which would break my husband's heart. I couldn't look Lindz in the eye during those long, long minutes. I didn't have the strength to tell him what had been happening to my body and therefore in my heart. Perhaps keeping silent meant that I could pretend the bleeding hadn't happened, to draw this out just a tiny bit longer.

Was it something I had done? Should I have stayed on the sofa instead of going to work? Was it that time I had lifted some small chairs onto a desk at school, when I'd momentarily forgotten who I was carrying inside? (Thankfully, this idea was later dispelled by a friend who told me that while in the same waiting period, she had gone for a simple walk which had turned into her and a group of friends getting lost and hiking over hills for miles. She remained pregnant and had a beautiful daughter. I had to let it sink in that my exertion was not the culprit; I didn't need to carry that guilt).

Right now, the thought of losing our babies was too raw. Doing the washing up was a welcome distraction while we waited for the result, then it was time to know.

Negative.

We'd lost them.

And our world seemed to melt in the moments following.

I sat on Lindz's lap and we both cried. Such a moment is incredibly hard for men too. Lindz was fully invested in becoming a daddy and his dreams had also just smashed painfully on the floor in front of him. We were listening to some music by a great friend of ours, the incredible songwriter Matt Redman, and didn't want to let each other go. Another song soon came on that we had sung over our little ones constantly in the run up to this moment, Breathe Life, by another friend, Andy Smith.

The words that had once held such hope almost instantly became a slap in the face after such appalling news.

You turned my ashes into beauty, turned my sorrow into joy, breathe life. You take these dry bones, make them stand, put a promise in my hand, breathe life.

In time, this song would come to hold a whole new meaning for us, as our journey would become about working towards our personal healing and wholeness as people, as well as trying to have a family and bring life into the world. Songs can be so powerful, in a positive or negative way, during such an ordeal.

That Sunday afternoon we had arranged to visit our friends the Delaneys, and we knew some other friends the Hawthornes would be there too. A house full of food and laughter always held the promise of a great afternoon. When the get together had been organised, we'd anticipated having exciting news to share with them. Lindz and I had discussed how we might announce our incredible news. Umm, guys, we've got something to tell you... I would tear up and get butterflies in my tummy with excitement just thinking about finally being able to share that news after so many years!

The events of that morning, however, meant that the day took a very different turn and we ended up sharing rather different news. We texted to say that we needed a bit of time to process the news together (and I needed time to reapply the make-up I'd cried off). Gemma came over and cried with us, Lynn texted a beautifully encouraging text, and finally we felt we had the strength to go and see everyone. I will never forget what followed. Anthony opened the door, grabbed us both in a big hug, kissed me on the head and said, "Sorry guys, we love you so much." He then ushered us into a room full of beautiful faces and lots of hugs. We didn't talk about what had happened then, instead we sat down and started to eat a little. We ended up smiling and even laughing at the jokes being shared. It was such balm for the soul!

Later we walked next door to Ivy Church for the evening service. By now we felt a little stronger and wanted to spend time with more church family. I opened the door and my brother-in-law James was praying from the front. I took one look at all the people sat in rows listening, and instead of gaining strength from it, I crumbled and ran out with Zoe in tow. I felt the familiar feelings of panic and despair wash over me and I sobbed. I was so grateful for Zoe being there, crying with me. Not many words were spoken, other than "Why?" from me and "I don't know, but you are so loved" from Zoe. It was all I needed at that time. Friends like these are so precious and that is why I am such an advocate for community. Friends who become family – they are the people around you who make you feel loved, accepted and understood, whatever's going on in your life. That day we would have SO preferred to be sharing different news, but looking back I am so grateful for that memory. The darkest of days can open up to allow in the most beautiful of interactions in the midst of the mess and the pain. When Lindz and I look back, that's all we see when we think of that day now. We were loved. There were glimmers and sparkles of hope in a hopeless situation.

As we moved further into our time of waiting and suffering, I noticed an incredible thing happening. I've since talked to many others who have suffered, and their response has been the same. Yes, there is the memory of the pain, but this is surpassed by the moments of care and love shown by the people who rallied around to give their support. This is so true for Lindz and I. We have "fond" memories of things people said and did, which "propped up" the thick blanket of agony that covered us and stopped it from smothering us.

There was my friend Jo, who popped over with a big bowl of comfort food and a hug – just what I needed when I could do nothing but sit and stare into space, or cry, or think awful thoughts about what was going on inside me. There was the time I sat in the garden, holding a pregnancy test way before we'd even started IVF. I let it drop to the ground as it showed up negative. My body had lied again, and I'd started to get excited about the changes, the lateness, the different pains I was feeling, only to have that hope cruelly snatched away by a stick. Gemma was there to hold my hand and support me. There were times when I was wearing my dressing gown, in my safe place, and needed to pour my heart out to someone, anyone, through deep sobs. Suddenly, there was a knock at the door and Zoe was there, speaking life and giving me the time and space I needed to get my agonising ramblings out. I remember thinking, "I look an absolute mess, what must she think of me?" then realising that friends don't think that way. They love you whether you have mascara on or not! Whether your eyes are red raw from crying or your hair is a frizzy mess. Again, I felt loved.

After all the pain of that Sunday, I woke up the following day and was thrown slightly. A strange thing happened. I was happier and more excited than I'd been for a long, long time! I thought about how many more lie-ins we'd get, how we'd possibly get at least one more holiday in before I was pregnant, of all the nights out we had ahead of us without having to find a babysitter. Then there was the extra money we suddenly had. I thought about all the time I still had to feel healthy and slim and not suffer from morning sickness or be incredibly grumpy with my husband. I thought about all the time my husband and I had to hang out together and how much work I could get done; the fun we could have; how spontaneous we could be… all these thoughts made me soar. It was a strange feeling – a bit like knowing you have a sentence to serve, then suddenly it's taken away and you're given your freedom. I wanted to celebrate this before it was taken away again. I actually enjoyed it!

We had been told this might happen, so we embraced the feelings while they lasted. Unfortunately, after a few short days of relief, deep despair clouded our lives again. Would this ever be over? I think back to this period of our lives sometimes and feel like it just didn't make any sense. Why should wanting to have a child cause so much pain? Why couldn't I just get over it and move on? I would tell myself, "This can't be as bad as losing someone you know and love, I'm sure," as if to reprimand myself. It's hard to "rate" pain, especially if that pain is invisible, hidden away. Because I didn't have a broken leg, or hadn't lost someone close to me, I began to feel that I had no right to feel so hurt. I chastised myself, telling myself to paste on a smile and get on with it. But I was being unfair, of course. The pain I felt waiting for children was so intense because to me, like many women, it seemed as though I was the only person suffering amongst a world of happy, fulfilled people.

During this time, I came to the very painful conclusion that the "ticking clock" feeling I was experiencing was very real and very painful when left unfulfilled. It's like having a time of grieving with nothing to show for your grief. There was no guarantee that Lindz and I would ever be parents. There was no fixed date in the future where we knew these clouds would clear. It was like walking in the wilderness with no clear path or signs to follow, no boundaries and no finish line. Being in the wilderness can bring a deep exhaustion, as you have nothing to help you navigate. You feel isolated and forgotten, like your life has been put on pause while everyone else's moves on. The dictionary definition of "wilderness" speaks of a "neglected or abandoned area"; a place that is "uncultivated, uninhabited and inhospitable". It's an accurate description of the place we found ourselves in. With no end in sight, every one of my senses told me that I was going to feel this way forever.

During times of waiting or grief, we need to show ourselves a lot of grace, never telling ourselves to simply get over it or snap out of it. We mustn't belittle our pain, or worse, minimise the pain of others who are going through similar challenges. People tried this with us. No doubt with good intentions, through wanting to help us get over it more quickly, peopled passed on encouraging stories about people they knew or had read about, adding limp promises at the end. "The same thing could happen to you…" or "As soon as you stop trying and relax, you will definitely get pregnant" and "If you go on the same diet this person followed then of course you will conceive." And on it went.

"Endings" such as these are just that: the end to someone else's story. Passing on information about other people's journeys can be very encouraging at times, but it's also wasted effort because their story is not our story. These things happened to other people and no two stories are the same; no two roads have the same twists and turns, smooth surfaces or potholes. We are all so different and our paths are different. I share this not because I'm angry that those "endings" were shared, but to illustrate how little people knew about helping others in pain. It was one of the reasons why we withdrew and stopped telling others what we were going through. We felt we needed to protect ourselves from the pat answers and platitudes that so easily fell from people's lips. Although it seems counterintuitive to hide rather than share pain, I wasn't willing to let everyone know how intense that pain was – the pain that I had no idea how to deal with myself.

I used to struggle with my sister being so open about her and her husband's journey to conceive. I wondered how on earth she could tell anyone and everyone she met about it, being honest about her feelings and sharing with virtual strangers. In fact, I used to will her to keep quiet! To protect that incredibly private personal information, and keep it between her and a close group of trusted family and friends, as we were doing. As time has gone on, however, I have seen the freedom she has brought to others as she has shared these truths. I am now seeing it too, as I share all that Lindz and I have walked through, and to some extent are still walking through. The truth is, it truly is a privilege to be able to say to someone, and mean it with your whole heart, "I'm sorry what you're going through is so hard and horrible. I understand and I'm with you." I learned a lot from my lovely, brave sister.

What used to be insanely private is now something I am ready to share with the world. It's no longer our secret to keep. It is, in fact, a beautiful scar; a healed wound from a battle Lindz and I courageously fought together, hand-in-hand and shoulder-to-shoulder with some of the most gorgeous people in our world. I once had a picture pop into my head of getting to Heaven and meeting Jesus for the first time. He looked at my scar, invisible to everyone else but obvious to Him, and cried. He cried because He knew all that I had walked through on earth and yet remained by His side, determined to see my faith grow, not shrink. I hold that picture so close to my heart and believe, one day, I will see those tears of pride for a girl who suffered and stayed! I definitely agree with Brené Brown that vulnerability with people is one of the most powerful roads to healing and contentment.

I have also chosen to share our life and story with people because there is still so much misunderstanding and misconception surrounding infertility and childlessness. Thankfully, there are people now doing incredible work to raise awareness of this kind of grief and provide support to parents who have suffered any kind of loss.

The charity The Mariposa Trust (widely known by its primary support division www.sayinggoodbye.org), for example, is doing incredible work in Parliament and in society, working to change laws and attitudes to recognise that these are longed-for children. The charity is supporting thousands of people every week through the pain of miscarriage, stillbirth, child loss and infertility. They also run Saying Goodbye services of remembrance for those who have lost a baby, and for those who are grieving never having had a child at all. Miscarriages are "lost children", not just a group of cells that have been ejected from a woman's body. These are children who were longed for, already loved, and are now being grieved over. The awareness being built around this kind of loss is much needed, as people who have suffered it need love, support and understanding.

I wrongly assumed that there was a hierarchy of loss. I believed for a long time that I was at the bottom of the suffering ladder because I hadn't carried a child myself – a thought I am sure I put upon myself, rather than it being imposed by others or society, but it felt very real to my broken heart. The truth is though, that we are in no position to categorise or quantify ours or another person's pain. Every person's journey is unique to them. And I hope that by sharing my story, it will contribute to a shift in people's thinking about how we empathise with those whose pain is perhaps hidden and invisible to others.

Looking back, I can see that this kind of hierarchical thinking affected me more than I realised at the time, and it still does to some extent. It's so easy to compare oneself to others then cast a judgement, but we must choose to give ourselves grace and allow the grieving process to happen.

Chapter Five

On particularly rough days, when I'm sure I can't possibly endure, I like to remind myself that my track record for getting through bad days so far is 100%, and that's pretty good!
–Unknown

Slowly but surely Lindz and I healed, emotionally as well as physically, and if there's one thing I learned over those years it is that you must be able to say *no* when your physical and mental health demands that you slow down and take time to care for yourself. For a while, I had been saying no more and more to going out with our younger friends, but when I stayed at home, I felt a stab of guilt and worried that I wasn't being a fun enough wife or friend. The pressure of saying *yes* to things that I didn't want to do was causing a strain that I could feel physically inside, but then I was plagued with thoughts that I wasn't good enough for Lindz, sometimes allowing myself to wish he had married someone else who could have made him happier and given him the child he was so desperate for.

One day, however, I had the revelation that I wasn't being boring at all. My deep need to be a mummy was producing these physical cravings and the desire to be at home and "nest". This was my heart's response to the deep desire to have a sleeping child upstairs. But there was no sleeping child upstairs, so no one understood why a seemingly healthy, happy person wasn't going out all the time and enjoying her "freedom".

Lindz is a full-on visionary extrovert and I adore that about him. He recharges and feels energised by seeing people and being out and about. I am a sociable introvert. I adore people and love socialising, but I have a cut-off point where I need quiet and space on my own to recharge my batteries. During this time of grief, my recharge time increased and far outweighed my capacity to socialise. After all these years, mine and Lindz's love for each other is far deeper for knowing and understanding these things about each other, but it wasn't always that way. It took us a long time to deeply love those differences!

I felt so cross with myself after that revelation. I felt like I had wasted so much energy on beating myself up, and Lindz and I had had so many disagreements, from minor ones to full-blown arguments, just because I didn't understand what I was feeling and how to communicate it without guilt and confusion getting in the way. Grief had violently pulled apart my identity and I was struggling to know who I was, let alone explain it to anyone else. Working through pain like this is a process. There are many ways to walk it out, and this will happen at a different pace for different people. How we tend to deal with things in general, and whether we have grieved deeply before, are factors that will affect how we respond. There is no right or wrong way to get through something like this, so the important thing is to take it one day at a time. We must give ourselves and others a safe place to talk through the pain with grace. If we try to avoid facing the issue by plastering on a false smile or putting a positive slant on everything, this can delay the healing process.

If you are worried about someone you love who is going through something like this, don't be scared to ask them how they are coping in a quiet, relaxing safe space. If they change the subject straight away, don't let that awkwardness stop you from being there for them the next time. Just let them know you're there to talk when they want, and although you may make mistakes, your heart is to be there for them. I recently heard someone share that as men don't always like to talk deeply about how they are feeling, simply asking a male friend/family member how they are feeling on a scale of 1-10 can help them to be honest with you, as they quickly quote a number and move on. The next time you check in, this can tell you what direction they are moving in – up, into freedom, or further down into despair – which in turn helps you to know how much to intervene and help them. Most times there will be little you can do physically to help someone through this, but as with any kind of grief, simply knowing there is someone there when you're ready to talk, who will love you through the tough parts, can help bring peace.

* * *

After having IVF treatment, you are told to leave at least one cycle (around a month) to allow your body to heal before having another round. However, we found, like many other couples, that we needed a bigger gap just to get our heads around it all. We left it around six months. As we started the treatment for a second time, we entered into it again full of hope. We believed again that it was *our* turn for success. The first time around had thrown up a lot of questions because we were walking into the unknown. Now, we knew what to expect, so we were feeling more positive and relaxed.

The injecting period was easier second time around, like riding a bike or brushing your teeth – it was just something that needed to be done each day and I ticked it off my list like a chore. In due course, egg retrieval day came. The road had been a little rocky and I'd had to attend a few appointments on my own as Lindz was working away. The nurses had wondered each time whether the eggs would be robust enough to retrieve, let alone fertilise, and they had nearly stopped the treatment three times. That had made me wobble so much. Waves of self-pity rushed over me and I felt like a small child sat alone on the bed. Each time, the nurse would pop out of the room to seek a third-party opinion, while I was left alone waiting, praying for good news but fearing the worst. When the nurse returned, the strain on her face told me that she knew the weight of her words. She knew that for so many women visiting the clinic, this was their last chance. But each time I was given the okay to keep going. The treatment was extended to give my eggs the fighting chance they needed. Thank you, Jesus.

This time, when the operation to place the eggs back in was over, I woke up super quick from the anaesthetic, so had to leave hospital straight away. I was gutted, as last time I'd had *loads* of gorgeous sleep and the best macaroni cheese ever! This time it felt like I was in and out within minutes, but the staff did a great job of looking after me and did everything they could to make me feel comfortable.

Being Christians, Lindz and I don't talk much about *coincidences*, preferring to call them *God-incidences*, and this round of IVF felt very different to the first. As soon as the operation was over, deep encouragements about how successful it was going to be seemed to come at us from every angle. Time and again things happened that felt out of this world – not your normal, run of the mill stuff. I understood these signs or words of comfort to mean that God was definitely going to bring about a pregnancy this time and I was flying! Here are just a couple of examples.

One day, I turned up at church early for a rehearsal, as I was singing at the front that morning. It was during the 17-day period that follows the operation, while we were waiting until we could do a pregnancy test. The previous night I'd had an incredibly vivid dream that had stayed with me all morning. In the dream, the Grim Reaper came into my room and I felt a rush of pure terror as he leaned over the bed to grab at my tummy. Although it was just a dream, the feelings were incredibly real and intense. It truly felt as though he was trying to steal my baby from me.

That morning at church there was a guest minister, a guy who interpreted dreams, so I thought I'd take advantage of the opportunity and share my dream with him. With my friend and church leader Anthony

Delaney standing alongside me for support, I asked the man what he thought my dream meant. He didn't know me from Adam, but shared the interpretation he felt God gave him: "You have new life inside of you and the enemy is trying to steal it." You don't have to believe in God to understand that this was a HUGE thing for me to hear at that moment. Both Anthony and I were struck dumb. There I was, fresh out of hospital, full of hope and, apparently, new life. This was it… it was our turn to be parents.

Similar things happened time and again to encourage my heart that we were indeed pregnant. The day before I was due to take my pregnancy test, I walked into church just in time to hear the words being sung, *joy comes in the morning*. Then, people who didn't know us told our friends, "This is strange, and a bit random, but we believe Lindz and Lucy are pregnant. Do you know if they are even trying?" Even though we had been incredibly private, and people knew nothing about what we were going through and the tiny lives I was carrying at that moment, the words kept coming.

I can't describe the joy I felt as I went out for a meal near the end of those 17 days. I was feeling everything that pregnant women describe at the beginning of conception: nausea, swelling, tenderness, tiredness, etc. I remember saying out loud, "If I'm not pregnant, then God can't be real with all the signs and wonders I've been given." I felt quite reprimanded when Lindz told me to be careful as I'd just spoken dangerous words. But I relished every one of those feelings, even though most of them were unpleasant and uncomfortable. I didn't mind in the slightest, I just wanted to savour the feeling of being *pregnant* at last!

In my diary, I wrote down the things that people had said, and wherever I turned I read or heard things that jumped out at me. I literally heard the words "you are pregnant" over and again in the 2-3 weeks leading up to the test, whether it came from people who didn't know us or even in TV programmes I watched. I was convinced I was pregnant, and this made the days of waiting feel more like the run up to Christmas as a kid. It was not at all like the first time around, where I'd spent so much time crying and questioning, full of fear.

On the morning I was due to take the pregnancy test, I took a shower, happy as Larry. Then I bled… a lot. This freaked me out more than the first time, because I'd had all these promises; so many words of encouragement. I felt like I'd been receiving fanfares from Heaven to declare the birth of this child, so how could it be going wrong? Panic set in and my breathing became rapid and shallow. Tears pricked my eyes and my thoughts became chaotic at the thought of what this could mean. I was completely out of control. The realisation crept over me that, if this had failed, not only would I have to live through the pain of losing our babies again, but I may have to question the very existence of God. How could I possibly believe in Him anymore, having received word after word, encouragement after encouragement, and so many freaky coincidences, yet still with no baby at the end of it? Nothing could have prepared me for what happened next.

It was near the beginning of September, 2010. I took the test, then Lindz and I busied ourselves again, trying not to think about the fact that in the next few minutes our lives would completely change. We would either experience immeasurable joy or be broken, perhaps beyond the point of no return.

It was the latter, and I didn't know what to do with myself.

I started to physically shake – first my hands, then my whole body. I had to be alone. The worst was happening. It had all gone wrong and I didn't know what to do about it. I knew that what I was feeling was pure terror as I considered the most frightening thought I'd ever had: that maybe God wasn't real and I was truly, utterly alone. That day I wrote in my journal:

"I know now I can cope without babies, but I can't cope without God."

Suddenly, in that moment, there was apparently no hope to speak of. No Creator to lovingly guide us through this crazy life, which had taken one nose-dive after another over the last few years. I have never felt so afraid. In those few seconds, it was as though I could see the whole journey laid out before me. My life had changed in a heartbeat from trying to conceive and have a beautiful pregnancy announcement, to trying to claw myself out of a pit that had opened up and swallowed me whole. Right now, in the midst of our bad news, it seemed impossible to climb out of that pit, so I retreated to be on my own and cried the deepest tears I'd ever cried. Lost hope – the saddest place of all.

My climb back to God was an incredibly slow process after that. I had to hold on to everything I had heard, read or experienced about Him in the past, and trust that these were real, even though everything in me denied it right now. It was a *choice* to get back to the surface, but I also kept slipping. Whenever the "rain" fell, the sides of that hole became muddy and slippery and I lost my grip. That hole became my cynical, desperately needy, sad friend for far longer than I would have wanted, but since leaving it, I've made myself a promise never to return. I can still visualise that place of isolation in my mind's eye and the knowledge of its existence is enough to keep me away.

There were times when I declared that if God was actually real, He must be downright mean. How could He have let our hopes be built up so much, with so many words about our future, only for them to be dashed so cruelly? Then there were the times when the cloud of hopelessness felt so heavy that I just didn't care about anything anymore. I started to realise that horrible beliefs had grown within me, like not believing anymore that prayer actually works, and not wanting others to experience the same disappointment that I had. When our church leader's son asked me whether his dad would be okay and return safely from a trip to earthquake-stricken Haiti, all he needed was a shallow reassurance – *Yes, he'll be fine* – and I couldn't even give him that. At that moment, it all felt like a lie. I wanted to say, "Well, actually no. There's a big possibility he won't return safely." Thankfully, someone else jumped in to reassure him before I could open my mouth. All my hope had gone. The colour had drained out of my world and music now felt like a clanging gong, every sound dull and annoying to my ears.

I had heard many times people say, "God brings good out of every situation". Whether said by a friend who wanted to be encouraging, or a Bible teacher, I began to despise these words. How, in any way, could this situation be *good*? But I was missing the point. I needed to understand (and thankfully, I eventually reached this conclusion) that He is able to bring good *out of* any situation, even though the situation itself is *not good*. I don't believe for a moment that God caused our suffering, and, after a few years, I began to feel more like He *trusted us* to go through it. We have now earned the right to a deep faith. We have been awarded the medal of holding on through the tough times; of making good choices; choices that would bring us through as stronger people, rather than becoming a cynical shell of our former selves. Now, our faith is a true faith – one that doesn't buckle under pressure; one that believes because it has seen, not because that's what we're supposed to do. I am so, so grateful for having been given something that money just can't buy, and now I always encourage others to hold on when going through similar pain and hopelessness. I don't know how people go through pain and grief without a faith in Jesus. I hear many stories of people who are trapped in pain, grief, disappointment, anger, guilt or unforgiveness many years after an event changed their lives, and this has affected their health and every relationship they've entered into. This is so sad because I believe there is a beautiful way out.

The truth is, there is *always* light at the end of the tunnel. For us, it was coming to a deeper place of faith in God *before* our promise arrived. Some will find the light and strength again along the way. For others, it will only return when they become parents or see an end to their problems. But the light *will* return if we are determined to hold on, even if it seems like the faintest candlelight and we persevere through gritted teeth and a cursing mouth. Of that, I am sure! As I write, I see a picture in my mind's eye of sailors in a storm, grabbing ropes and tying them tightly around themselves, physically attaching themselves to the ship as it pitches and rolls under the weight of wind and rain. When we are suffering, we each need to find our safe place and tether ourselves securely to it, determined not to allow our circumstances to take us under. You *will* get through this.

With the benefit of hindsight, I can see the issues so clearly, but at this point in our story I didn't realise that our challenges were far from over and that there were some incredibly hard days to come. And these, I believe, are what brought about the biggest changes in the long run.

When I think of the pain now, I look back and picture myself like one of those little wooden children's toys where you press the base and the figure crumples in a heap. I was in a slump of hopelessness, as the following extracts from my diary show. It was often very hard for me to put into words the true extent of my grief.

"What is this pain? I just watched *Slumdog Millionaire* with Zoe and Anthony and spent the whole journey home shouting 'WHY, GOD, WHY?' at the top of my lungs, with tears pouring down my cheeks. Lindz and I have SO much love and life to give these children... WHERE ARE THEY??!!

I have this horrible feeling, deep down, that our children are all over the world and they've been stolen. Where are they? How do we find or rescue them? These four walls feel like they are crushing me right now. I'm so broken and I don't know what I can do to fix it. Where has my hope gone? I don't know if I'll ever find happiness again.

WHERE ARE MY BABIES? MY HEART IS BREAKING."

"We've just been to a family wedding. Chris and Gemma came up to us saying they needed to talk, and could we all go into the next room. I panicked. I just knew they were going to tell us they were pregnant, but my battered heart couldn't take it. We went in there just before them and I said over and over to Lindz like a mad woman, 'I can't take this, please make it stop. I don't think I can do this now, please make it stop, Lindz, please make it stop!' Of course, it didn't stop, and they told us. I remember thinking, *I'm trying to hold back a panic attack and you're crying Gemma, telling us you've had a hard time waiting for this news. We have been waiting for years and we're still no closer! I don't know how much more of this I can take.*"

"Okay, so EVERYONE is pregnant now. Thank goodness Hannah is still around. If Hannah tells me she's pregnant, then that's it – everyone close to me will be either pregnant or already parents. Where the heck do I go now?"

(Hannah fell pregnant just one month after that diary entry).

"What a flipping hard couple of weeks. First, I lost it and had panic attacks twice. One was in Morrisons. I had to abandon my trolley full of shopping and drove to Caz's house praying she'd be there. They pulled up outside just as I did! I walked in and sobbed. I know I'm going through the pain of believing that I may *never* have my own child; may never have a little person who looks like Lindz or me. It's always been one of my biggest fears and here I am, having to face it head on. But now

I'm here, it's not quite as big and scary as I thought it would be, and I am starting to believe I can get through this day by day. I guess maybe people are right when they say God gives you the grace you need, as you need it. 'My grace is sufficient for you, for my power is made perfect in your weakness.' (2 Corinthians 12:9)."

and...

"The deep sadness has returned. It's weighing me down like a heavy cloak or a large bag. I feel so low, to the point where I'm actually stooping my shoulders and physically unable to lift my head. I'm trying to stay busy, to not think about it, but the tiniest of reminders makes my world comes crashing down again. I've felt utterly alone in it this time. Lindz has been away loads. Caz has just adopted her precious, beautiful daughter, Jessica. Jane is starting out on this hideous adventure. Gemma's just had her second baby. Libby's gone. The Hawthornes, Clarks and Delaneys have all just been away... I'm totally alone.

But the very next day...

"Dave Clark just phoned me and asked me some honest questions, making me talk. I couldn't believe how much I finally felt loved and understood in this. Every time I think I may never hold a tiny person that looks like Lindz, I die again, and the pain overwhelms."

I decided to include the diary entry above, not to shame anyone for not being around at that time – I know full well how busy life can be and that people have families and other commitments – but to show how one phone call can change all of that. What a blessing one kind word is from a close friend at the right time.

It's good to check ourselves regularly and ask, "Who am I looking after or looking out for?" There will always be those around us who are going through their own deep sadness and need us to pick up the phone, drop them a quick text to say we're thinking of them, or take them out for lunch and maybe ask the hard questions, which they may or may not be ready for. But it is SO good to check in; to give people the opportunity to talk about whatever they want, without us butting in all the time with our own advice. You have much more to give to people who are struggling than you think.

Chapter Six

Even when we are going through a difficult time ourselves, we can still give the gift of true empathy to others during their hard times.

I continued to experience a rollercoaster of highs and lows, all the time questioning, “Is God *really* real? Will I ever fully trust Him again?” There was so much going on inside of me that I couldn’t share with others.

One year, Lindz’s family came to ours for Christmas. It was something we had dreamed of since getting married, as each year we would pack the whole of Christmas into our car and make the trip to either Bristol or London for a few days. Then we’d pack up everything again and go to the other parents before travelling home to a cold house and a sad, dying Christmas tree. This year it was our turn to host.

I was so excited to have everyone there and pleased not have to leave my beautifully decorated, cosy home. I started the Christmas dinner and soon found myself alone in the kitchen. I was struggling a little, as I had never cooked a full Christmas dinner for so many on my own before. Then Lindz came in and noticed that the potatoes weren’t cooking as evenly as he would have liked, which led to a nasty comment from him and me getting angry and snapping back at him. I was struggling to pull everything together on time, but also nursing a broken heart, and I had a tendency to lose my temper or get offended at the smallest of things, which I did right then. Poor Lindz.

Unfortunately, his parents heard my little outburst and took it to mean I needed some space, so they did the one thing I didn’t want them to do right then. They put on their coats and suggested they go for a walk. Actually, the last thing I needed was some space, I needed some help with the cooking. I even suggested that some help would be a better alternative, but the walk still went ahead. I understood what they must have been thinking, *They need to work things out. We'll just get in the way if we say or do anything...* but unfortunately, that was almost everyone's viewpoint at the time, and I just felt terribly lost and alone. Lindz was quick to join them too, as I was irritating him so much.

I looked through the house as they disappeared and found everyone else sitting around a beautiful fire, laughing and relaxing together, and it was just too much. I went down into the cellar and sobbed. I hugged my knees tightly and sobbed silent tears, so as to not draw attention to myself. I was so fed up with being left alone to deal with this, or being expected to "get over it" because I am generally seen as a strong person. I had begun to see that I needed help, and it felt like all I was getting was people retreating from me, feeling awkward, or not understanding how raw I felt inside. That day turned out well in the end, but I never fully engaged, and every bit of banter directed towards me just burned into my heart. I was a broken girl and I knew it would take a lot longer than I'd like to put me back together.

Mum and Dad came over quite soon after the failed IVF and a similar thing happened. Mum was talking about my sister, Sarah, offloading her problems onto my flimsy, shaky shoulders and I just broke. I shouted something quite mean as my patience had completely run out. Very soon after, Lindz said something insensitive and I snapped. I left the house, walked the 200 metres or so to our local park, ran down the steps and sat on the bottom one, crying and praying over and over, "God, please would you be real right now and send someone to talk to me? Anyone, please just let SOMEONE ask me how I am, why I'm crying, why I'm so desperate." And He did! At that moment a dog trotted by and a woman's voice called out, "Lucy, come here!" which obviously made me jump. Then the lady spotted me sitting there crying and stopped to ask if I was okay. We chatted and I was completely honest with her. I don't think I made much of an impact on her life, but she certainly changed mine that day. That was most definitely an answered prayer and it lit a tiny flame back in my heart. I was on my way home.

We can feel so ashamed of suffering, and guilty for asking questions of ourselves over and again. Ours were, "why us?", "are we not good enough?" and "what have we done wrong?" All impossible questions. It was easy to assume that our thoughts, attitudes, speech and behaviour were in some way to blame for this. The irony that our family had looked after, sacrificed for, and unconditionally loved 107 of the most beautiful, difficult, damaged children, yet my sister and I could not conceive, was not lost on me. The pain I saw my parents go through, especially my beautifully emotional mum, was heart breaking at times. I know she tried to keep it together for our sake, but when she let down her guard and her pain came out, it shook me. There were times when mine and Lindz's personal pain was so intense that it seemed to be ours alone, eclipsing all others, and I was unaware of how much it was also affecting my parents and in-laws.

Mum shared in her church one Sunday morning, through tears, that her daughter had just suffered her second miscarriage through IVF treatment and asked for their prayers to help us all through it. I should have been there for Mum at this hard time, but instead, I was livid. There were some people in the church I would have felt comfortable about knowing this information, but I was acutely aware of the many others – especially the newer faces and names, and the people we didn't know at all who were maybe visiting – who I didn't want to know what we were going through. Our private misery and humiliation had suddenly been thrust into the public domain, becoming a thing to be discussed and mused over by strangers. I, in particular was desperate to avoid this, afraid of it even. I have come to understand, however, that this was how Mum needed to deal with *her* grief, so I had to choose to forgive and move on. I could not afford to walk in any more pain, especially that of unforgiveness. Mum shared her pain and so got the support she needed, which was in fact, a wise thing to do. Over the years I'd allowed myself to become so protective over what was happening to us that I'd forgotten that it was hurting those close to us too. It made me pretty useless at bringing the comfort, understanding or clarity they needed at that time.

It's SO powerful to be able to speak to someone who understands the journey we are on, who will just listen when we're hurting and need to talk. I was useless with helping others because I kept everyone at arm's length, yet if I'd allowed people to come close, we could have helped each other. Even when we are going through a difficult time ourselves, we can still give the gift of true empathy to others during their hard times. Empathy is "the ability to understand and share the feelings of others". I often felt that I received more pity than understanding. I battled between strong waves of pride and despair. That people could pity us pushed my true feelings deeper and deeper into the abyss that contained my broken heart. If I never talked about it, maybe it would all just go away. What I really needed was understanding.

Then, suddenly I tasted empathy in the form of a friend I hadn't seen for a while when we got talking at her brother's wedding. She had been going through exactly the same thing as me and spoke in such a refreshingly honest way about bleeding in the shower during her IVF treatment, and about how it felt to know she was losing her babies. She was the first person I'd connected with on this long journey who just *got it*. I didn't want the conversation to end and wished we'd been somewhere more private. What she gave me in those snatched moments was a glimpse of the person I had been before this. The realisation that I wasn't completely messed up – there was in fact a very normal human being inside my distressed body – and one day, this would no longer be who I was, but rather something I had walked through that had subsequently made me stronger. As yet, I still couldn't see beyond the day-to-day battle, but I had been thrown a lifeline, given a "get out of jail free" card I could file away for use at a later date. My friend was okay now, she had children and was functioning beautifully in society. There was hope.

There are forums all over the internet that discuss the challenges of infertility. Some of them can provide real connection, empathy even, and be a source of comfort to many, but as I ventured into this world most of what I found was people expressing their pain. For me, there were no answers to be found and no hope offered, just negative speech. Quite quickly this dialogue began to bring me down, so I made a choice to avoid hanging out there. I knew that what Lindz and I needed most were people around us that we could be real with. People who had walked similar paths and survived. People who had hard-won wisdom that we could learn from. I have now learned to surround myself with strong women who bring wisdom, clarity and encouragement. Those who know to offer a cuddle and a nod during the difficult times, instead of wallowing with me in the pain. This is far better for the soul.

I began to meet more and more people who had gone through some kind of deep pain, survived and were now thriving, and slowly it dawned on me that this was a journey of choices. Did I want this pain to define me? Or did I want to be free from it, even if I *never* had a child? Every time I let my mind dwell on the pain, I felt the comforting stab of self-pity and realised that I was *choosing* to stay down, *choosing* to lose the fight. Every time I chose to be mindful of what I was thinking and direct my thoughts towards more positive things, I was winning.

I thought back to an event from several years before. After returning home from a really fun, family holiday, my boyfriend at the time (who I adored) dumped me very suddenly, when I was really looking forward to seeing him again. I didn't see it coming and couldn't believe it, as I had been planning my future with him. I was angry at what had been stolen from me. While I sat miserably staring at the walls of my room, nursing a broken heart and listening to sad songs on repeat (why did I do that to myself?!) I read something that directed me to a verse in the Bible. These words have since become some of the most powerful ones I've used to keep me strong and confident.

"...we take captive every thought to make it obedient to Christ." (2 Corinthians 10:5)

This verse suddenly came alive to me. I'm quite a visual person, so I decided there and then to act out physically "grabbing" those thoughts from my head, scrunching them up like an unwanted sheet of paper, and throwing them away. I did this many times that day, over and again, whenever I forgot myself and allowed my thoughts to dwell on the sadness. By the end of the day I noticed something: I didn't have to do it very often and the sadness was not nearly as strong as it had been. I went from experiencing the pain of losing someone I thought I'd one day marry to being absolutely fine in less than three days!

This taught me an incredible lesson – one that I now needed to revisit – our thoughts, when allowed to develop negatively, can be a powerful force that keep us knocked down, trapped in our pit of pain. Looking back, I realise that I actually "thought" my way into freedom and I really believe that anyone can do the same when they know how. I believe I have the authority to make that statement because only a few years previously, throwing pity parties and camping in them for a long time was my normal. I knew I had stumbled across something that would serve me well in years to come, something that would bring me back from the edge and keep me sane. Someone put it simply and profoundly when they said, "Your mind is a powerful thing. When you fill it with positive thoughts, your life will start to change."

It is said that positive people don't *have* a good day, they *make* a good day. When it comes to major life choices and our general mental wellbeing, cultivating positive thoughts is vital. I'm not talking here about the kind of positivity one might find in a gung-ho self-help book, or a positivity that ignores reality, but a gritty, day-to-day resilience based on truth, which grows out of the good choices we make. Choosing to be grateful, for example, can be an incredibly powerful force in bringing positivity into our daily lives. You may be living through a time of great sadness, but there will always be something, however small, that you can choose to be grateful for.

Over time, thankfulness and positivity will change your focus, bring new experiences and change your perspective. Maybe you are experiencing a lot of fear right now, or believe that you are just not good enough. How about writing a list of what you *can do* rather than dwelling on what you *can't*? This list may be a hard one to write when you're feeling low, so give yourself grace and maybe wait until you are feeling a little better one day. When you can see written in front of you the things you are good at, then new obstacles aren't nearly as scary as they seem. You may even feel your limitations lifting and new possibilities growing inside of you.

There are many other ways you can build positivity into your life. It might sound too simple or trite but smiling more actually does work. Even smiling to yourself in the comfort of your own home can change how you feel on the inside. Remember that sadness and suffering will come, but you have hope walking alongside. We must not fear the gamut of emotions the body can throw our way. In fact, every emotion is essential and significant. To be a rounded person and have a depth of understanding of life, we must embrace the bad and the good as each shape us in different ways.

Life feels so much lighter and happier when we speak positively. It's not always easy to do, in fact on hard days it's the last thing we want to do, but we should see it as a muscle that needs to be exercised and strengthened. Breaking habits and building new ones takes time and determination, but it is totally possible. If there is something in your life right now that you're serious about changing but can't seem to shake, write down a few sentences about what you want to see change in you. Don't focus on the negatives, focus on the person you will become. Speak these words out loud daily, a few times if you can, and see how your heart begins to change and your mind begins to think differently. Our hearts and minds are strong and we have been built for survival, even in times of immense pain and stretching, so this is so worth the investment. Positive declarations have played a huge part in my personal recovery and have brought back the colour where there were only shades of grey.

If you are struggling, or have struggled like me, I want to tell you that it's okay to question God too. He promises to be our Father and it's okay to aim your frustrations at Him and ask for answers. He is not offended by your frustration or your doubt. He is a safe place and you can share with Him the areas of your life where you are hurting most. You can talk to Him about what is making you fed up and causing you pain. By being brutally honest with God, I learned to trust again: to trust Him, to trust my heart, to trust people and allow them back into my life and journey. I am so grateful to have trust firmly back in place in my life – it was definitely something worth fighting for. One amazing side effect of this is that I don't worry like I used to. Of course, at times I get frustrated, but I don't sweat the small stuff as much anymore.

Surely peace is a state of mind worth giving everything for? If we are serious about getting free, getting well, getting fit or anything else, then we will move mountains to achieve it. That's the place Lindz and I eventually arrived at. Yes, we had days where we hated every moment of what life was throwing at us, but as the years progressed, taking one mini-step forward after another, we were becoming two very determined people who were committed to personal change, even if our circumstances didn't alter. Because our journey seemed to have no end, we needed to forge ways of coping with our "normal". Had we not chosen the route of positivity and gratefulness for what we did have, we would have been stuck in perpetual pain. Growing up I had resorted to the pity party far too often, so I had to really work at being resilient and committed to positivity. It didn't come naturally, but that's why I'm stressing its importance. If it can work for someone like me, it can work for you.

As a result of a change of thinking, which led to a change of attitude, the third time we went through IVF felt very different to the previous times. My parents very kindly offered to pay for it, as we no longer qualified for free treatment. It was a generous offer, as it can be incredibly expensive. We started down that well-worn road again and sat in the same waiting rooms, same treatment rooms, and underwent the same blood tests – this time as paying customers – and heard the same concerns, this time made harder by the fact that Lindz was working away and couldn't make all the appointments.

"I'm afraid we can't see many follicles forming, and the ones that are there aren't growing quickly enough…"

"If this carries on, you may not be able to have any eggs extracted, which means there won't be any to fertilise and implant."

When the nurses said these words to me, they were hard to hear but didn't floor me as they would have previously. I was renewed. My heart was healing and I felt stronger than ever. So, this time the bad news was followed by a feeling of peace rather than dread, and an inner knowledge that we would be okay. This was VERY different from before. Don't get me wrong, it hurt me deeply because we still desperately wanted children and each treatment felt like our last chance, but the circumstances didn't floor us like they did before.

However, our worst fears concerning the IVF were quickly confirmed: they could not harvest enough eggs and we were told it would be a waste of money to continue. The treatment stopped immediately, and the rest of our payment was refunded… just like that. It was a formality, but to me it felt like we were being told, "Take this slip of paper to the lady at the desk, then your chance of having a family, including all your dreams and hopes for the future will be refunded. You're free to take this horrendous issue home with you to deal with as you wish. Goodbye."

We subsequently had a meeting with the head surgeon who talked mostly about my egg production slowing down, but didn't rule out us being able to have children naturally in the future – though he did say he wouldn't take us through any more treatment as it would be unfair to take our money. Walking out of that meeting, I had "heard" that the door was now closed – we'd need to explore an alternative route to having children, whereas Lindz took away from this "never say never". Two very different viewpoints! The reality was, we had been told that our journey with IVF should end, as it was never going to be successful. I can't recall in detail the days following that huge statement as I didn't record them in my journal – as though writing them down would have made them too real. But the truth was, they *were real*. Sadly, I seemed to be running out of eggs faster than other people. So, life continued on as it had. We went back to work, we socialised, we cooked, we cleaned, and we tried to get on, knowing that our chances of ever having a child were getting slimmer and slimmer with each passing day.

Life often has a strange way of pulling the rug, flipping us onto the floor one day, then throwing the most exciting things our way the next. Nic, who had been with me in BlushUK and was now singing with Lindz in

LZ7, fell pregnant which was good news for more than one reason. First, I knew she would embrace this and be an incredible mum, and second, quite selfishly, I knew it would open up the way for me to sing for LZ7. This was a dream I'd had since leaving BlushUK, maybe even since Lindz had set up the band all those years ago. I loved, and still love, LZ7 with all my heart. I loved travelling with Lindz and the boys and felt like this was *just* what I needed to take my mind off the constant nagging emptiness. It felt so much easier as the conversation very rarely revolved around children, nappies, little person cuddles etc. It was a real relief to have some banter and not have to think too hard. I was still taking photographs and doing a bit of supply teaching, but I was also spending weekends on the road, traveling all around Europe and eventually to New Zealand, performing, interviewing, getting to represent the band I so loved. Things could not have got much better than they were at this time.

My first proper gig with LZ7 was at the Soul Survivor festival at Shepton Mallet. I was, of course, pretty nervous. I had so much to prove being the new girl, but I was also a seasoned performer. Over the years I had performed in the same venue with STORM, BlushUK and now LZ7. The nerves began to grow as I started to do my hair and make-up in my sister-in-law's on-site caravan. They were dancing around like angry butterflies who couldn't find the exit.

My sister, Gemma, was there and in a few short minutes I would regret choosing a warm caravan over the toilet block we were offered by the venue to get ready in. Gemma suddenly felt ill and began throwing up into one of their salad bowls, poor thing! I was due on stage in less time than I had, and my sister really needed my help. I am incredibly ashamed to say that I ended up finding a way for her to prop herself over the bowl and called Chris, her husband, to come back as quickly as possible to take over. I rushed through my hair and make-up while apologising over 50 times then ran off to perform. Luckily, she forgave me, the gig went great, and I felt that beautiful feeling again that I'd always felt performing. I was alive and where I was supposed to be.

LZ7 was just what I needed while feeling so delicate. Lindz and Nathan shouldered most of the responsibilities, I just had to get there, look pretty and sing well. I could do that for now and I was so grateful for this respite from real life. I was thankful for the return of laughter – something I hadn't experienced for a while. Life had become so heavy, it was beautiful just to be able to belly laugh at the jokes and impressions the boys did to pass the hours. This, combined with photography, made for enough to keep my mind occupied.

It is said that a change is as good as a holiday, and I am so grateful to God that He gave me that time to heal, and for the many relationships I formed over that time. It was so good for the soul. Maybe there is something you need to change right now, or maybe it would help to take up a hobby – something that will bring you peace, distraction, a glimmer of a smile even, and the hope that there is light at the end of the tunnel.

Chapter Seven

Don't give up on the person you're becoming.

Conversations between Lindz and I tentatively began to touch on the idea of adoption. We had talked about possibly adopting at the start of our marriage, so this wasn't a shock. The difficult bit was accepting that it would be coming before we'd had our own children not after. But now, with other avenues closing around us, we felt caged in, backed into a corner even, like adoption was our only option if we wanted to have children. Unfortunately, with these conversations came the usual extremes of desperation I seemed to swing between. Now that we had touched upon a possible solution, I wanted it to happen right there and then, so I could have the family I was so desperate for. But nothing is ever that easy, there was another process to go through and it had to begin somewhere.

We decided to go ahead and gather information. We had nothing to lose by doing this, so Lindz and I went to an official meeting that outlined the adoption process and gave us sufficient information to make the hard decision of whether we really wanted to adopt or not. The thought of adopting someone else's child can seem overwhelming to some, especially if you were able to get pregnant and have your own children with no problems. It can seem such an alien thought, but here we were, entering into this arena – and not for purely altruistic reasons, to give a home to a child who didn't have one, but because we were desperate for someone to help us achieve our goal of having a family. This, of course, threw up many questions and many prayers were said, sometimes forced through gritted teeth, but said, nonetheless.

When I was young, I lived believing that "family" meant the people who lived in the same house as me. As my parents fostered more and more children, my definition of family grew larger; and as numerous friends spent time in our home it grew wider still, to the point where family meant the people who found a room in our hearts, not just our home. The truth is, "family" encompasses those people we do life with and feel connected to; those who are able to bring us joy and a smile with only a small comment or joke. It is those wonderful people that we can completely "be ourselves" around. There is something incredibly powerful about allowing the people around us to see more deeply into our lives. It can be quite terrifying at times, to be honest, and vulnerable, but with that comes healing and an unmovable knowledge that we are loved, which is the most wonderful thing of all. That is why, deep down, I knew that if we adopted a child we would be able to love them without limits.

By now we were beginning to understand that this journey belonged to us – we didn't accidentally fall into it or take a wrong turn. We needed to make peace with it and learn to navigate our new normal, thriving where we were at. The way I describe it now is that adoption was God's Plan A for us all along. We just didn't know it at the time, so we often felt like we'd taken a wrong turn or somehow missed what we were supposed to do to build a family. Thankfully, by now I owned the deep belief that nothing in the past had been our fault, as some people had wrongly hinted at during the hard time of waiting.

Before you think I had now risen above all the pain, there were still days when life felt so unfair. I still looked at friends who had fallen pregnant and apparently sailed through having one, two then three children, and asked, "Why me, God? What I have done that is so awful?" I would see pictures of family holidays or weekends filled with walks, picnics, fun and smiles, and feel it was unfair that my dreams had been smashed to smithereens. The longer time ticked away, the more I felt it was unfair that our children, if we had any, would have older parents, and possibly not have us around for as long as their friends' parents. Also, our parents would have less time with their longed-for grandchildren… the list went on. Yet, I knew that dwelling on such negative thoughts would kill me, so I chose to move past them and not try to second-guess our future.

I believed we had started on the home run now:

The adoption process = family = happy Lucy and Lindz.

Surely, that's how it happens? Naïvely, I thought we'd been through the worst of the journey, but little did I know, the hardest part was just around the corner: full… blown… grief.

As we began the process of adoption, I sensed that the pain of not having our own children was going to stay with me forever if I didn't do something about it. Every so often, Lindz would ask the question of whether we should try IVF one last time, before it was too late, just in case. We'd sat there and heard the doctor speak the same words, but being such different personalities, I had heard it as a realist and decided we need to change tack – not give up, but not put ourselves through unnecessary heartbreak if the medical professionals were so certain it wouldn't work. Lindz, being the incredibly positive person he is, felt the door wasn't completely shut. It was conversations like these and the pain of seeing babies and small children under the age of three (the age we were told our adopted child would likely be) that made me decide: I had to do something about this pain and the deep desire to have and hold my own child.

But what on earth could I do?

The trigger was sitting with my lovely friend Jan in the Trafford Centre near Christmas, a few months before we started the adoption process.

We were watching our church choir present a Christmas carol concert in the middle of the eating area. It was amazing to be there and a privilege to have such a prominent stage at such a busy time of the year. However, being somewhere this public wasn't something I did a lot and I struggled seeing so many children out and about in the run up to Christmas. Mothers with prams were out in force and I was bombarded by gorgeous little children cooing and gurgling, baby talking and "floppy" walking. With their chubby little hands and big eyes, all smiles and giggles, it was enough to melt anyone's heart.

As I sat watching, with uneaten food in front of me, Jan looked at me and asked how I was. She was a mother figure to me, always so kind and loving me through the worst. As soon as she expressed her care, my shoulders slumped and my head fell onto her shoulder. I sobbed a sad, silent sob. I was broken and I didn't want to do this anymore. I had been trying so hard to be positive, to speak well, and to get on with enjoying life, but the truth was, I was doing it all in my own strength, pretending and smiling because that's what people wanted to see. They didn't want to see my pain stretching on and on like this. In so many ways I felt much stronger, yet in many others I was still so broken. There were times when I just didn't know how to do life anymore, and it was the realisation of this that helped me to take action – action that might confuse some: I fully surrendered.

The next day, I sat at home slumped on my sofa and I surrendered everything I had to God. I told Him out loud that I didn't care anymore what happened to me. I couldn't live with this ache any longer, feeling so different from everyone around me. I told Him that I needed to be okay with never having biological children of my own, or having any children at all; that I was prepared to go through whatever was needed to pull off that sticking plaster and live with full joy and strength again. I relinquished all control and told God that it was His turn now. I had done everything I could on my own and my situation had not improved, so now I needed Him more than I ever had before. The pain had become like a disease in my soul, spreading out of control. Though I was stronger in so many ways, I needed the root of that pain to be dug out and removed forever. Anyone with an ounce of gardening knowledge will understand that to remove a deeply embedded root will be a violent extraction. It's not easy to dislocate and rip out something that has made its home somewhere it shouldn't be. And that is exactly what it was. This was not going to be a walk in the park.

Soon after, it came: a Tsunami of pain.

Over the next few days it ripped through me from the very depths of my being, like I'd never experienced before. No diversion tactic in my well-rehearsed book could stop it. This was real. There was so much crying. Some days I held my knees and rocked, staring at nothing in particular. Other days, I drove the car, shouting and screaming as I did, not caring who saw this demented woman releasing all of her hurt and anger. Every time I let it out, I would feel a tiny bit better. It was like lifting the lid on a pressure cooker, just a touch. I read up about grief, listened to podcasts, prayed, asked God to help me through, and spoke positive words with trembling lips. I allowed myself the hard times – I didn't try to brush them away or walk around them. I gave myself the space and grace I needed to do this. And, slowly but surely, I did it – or rather WE did it. I came through the other side of grief in one piece, seeing a different path for my life. One that had strength, success, freedom… joy, even. I was beginning to visualise all of this without the children I so dearly wanted. That was certainly not enjoyable, but I was aware of God walking with me, every step of the way.

In reply to the retrospective question of, "Why did God allow this to happen?" I can say with complete certainty that He didn't make it happen but in His amazing grace He used it to see us grow. I can also assuredly say that He stepped right into our mess and walked ever so closely beside us. There were days when my body ached from so much crying and I just needed a simple hug. God's presence was real, and I smiled each time I thought of Him, as if I was looking straight into the mighty creator's eyes. Without this time, I wouldn't be the person I am today. Before this, I often found myself looking over my shoulder, asking "what if?" rather than "what could be?" and I finally emerged from the gloom into a place of sunshine and open fields.

Freedom, beauty and joy were all returning, and in excess. I felt so unworthy. I had spent years effectively cursing at God, holding Him accountable for my pain, yet now He was removing so much of that and putting a goofy smile on my face for all to see. The disease of "want", of "dissatisfaction" was being removed at its very root and the musical soundtrack to my life, which so often played in my head, was sounding more major notes than minor. I could breathe deeply without it hurting. I could stand tall without sagging under the weight of shame. I had hope again, knowing with everything in me that God was real and that, one day, I would be useful once more, whether or not I became a mother. I also became resolute in my heart that I would not only help others who were going through this to gain the freedom I was now feeling, but I would never live life again looking over my shoulder at those despicable "what ifs". There are memories and feelings that I believe will never leave me, as people often say, and I agree. Moving through grief doesn't necessarily take you back to how things were before, it just helps you to live your new normal with peace, looking forward not just backward.

I view the after-effects of pain like a scar, seen visibly on the skin. When you are walking through the pain, you are tending to an open wound – a malady you're constantly aware of for most of your waking hours. You don't want anything near it that could cause more discomfort. Over time, the wound heals, but if knocked there is still the reminder of what was there. Some days, even now, what Lindz and I walked through can cause some tears to fall, but now there is a difference: I think about how far I have come, and my heart becomes grateful again; the tears dry, and my smile reappears.

Practically and emotionally, there are many things you have to lay aside when you don't carry your own children. A big issue for both Lindz and I was not having a child who looked like us, and who carried our genes. Then there were other things that, as a woman, plagued me. Breastfeeding was a big one. Not to be able to experience that bond between mother and child was very hard. I'm sure it's a beautiful thing. I do realise that there are many mothers who can't breastfeed for a variety of reasons, and that those brave women have to work through this issue too. Then, I missed being able to take "the" pregnancy test – the one where I saw the blue line appear and could get excited about planning to tell our parents and anyone else who would listen! I missed out on watching that baby growing inside me, holding Lindz's hand over my belly as our little one kicked me for the first time. I missed the joy of discovering whether we were having a boy or a girl, then planning the nursery. I couldn't experience the tiny newborn phase, where you just stare at your child for hours while they do absolutely nothing and you get to watch morning TV and ignore all the housework that needs doing. Then there is missing out on taking thousands of photos of the cute little faces they pull.

But I can also choose to turn this around and be thankful that I have not experienced swollen ankles, tender breasts, morning sickness, growing in size and the possible insecurity that comes with one's body changing so completely. Then there is the sleep deprivation I've heard so much about and the utter exhaustion of this pulling me away from Lindz for a while. Strangely, I now feel quite relieved that I have never gone through this, while feeling proud of the brave women who have. I'm proud of every single woman who has experienced sleep deprivation, being woken constantly through the night by a hungry baby, so intense that it caused out-of-body experiences and a brain fuzz that can only be explained by a massive surge of hormones. I'm proud of the women who have felt pain, weakness and insecurity, yet have gotten up and carried on in the midst of that haze to care for the tiny life they have fallen so utterly, completely in love with. These women, I salute you. I used to envy you, but now I carry pride and a familiar knowledge of that deep, deep love a mother has. The love that means she will do ANYTHING to protect and nurture her child.

The daily nag of pain was at last drifting from my heart and I felt strong enough to get ready for our next adventure: adoption. I chose to save speaking about this until the end of the book, as dealing with the issues of adoption and infertility simultaneously could have been overwhelming for anyone who is hurting and waiting for their own child. Some couples have remained childless as the thought of adoption is too overwhelming for them. Some have adopted, then gone on to have birth children afterwards. Everyone's journey is so different, and everyone has to choose their own path.[4]

As you've read, Lindz and I had to go through a process to get to the place where we were okay with adoption and no longer pursued having our own children. But how did we do it? Although there have been examples of how we walked through each phase throughout the book, there are a few more things I would like to pass on, which made a huge difference to us as a couple and the final outcome we are now walking in.

I always said that while I had Lindz by my side, I could cope what whatever was being thrown our way. Sadly, I know that this is not the

4. I have written another book which explains in depth the adoption process, and how it has affected and changed our family.

case for every couple and statistics show that couples are three times more likely to break up after failed fertility treatment. We chose never to pin the blame on each other or see the other person as the enemy in our story. This turned out to be a very powerful thing as it helped us to trust one another with our deepest thoughts and feelings. When the tears flow, you need to feel that you are in a safe place, and can share anything with your other half. It is devastating for both of you to not have the family you have dreamed of, and you will probably deal with the pain very differently, but standing together, shoulder to shoulder through the pain, will make you stronger in the long run.

Next, Lindz and I found that having a few trusted friends around us who knew what we were walking through, and who we could turn to for support, helped ease some of the shame and isolation we felt. I mentioned earlier that I found it helpful to not spend time in online forums about infertility. As soon as I walked into that minefield of oversharing, I felt completely overwhelmed. There was so much pain there that it inevitably caused me feelings of self-pity. Rather than soak up this negativity, Lindz and I made an effort to look for the positive. If you feed your mind with the wrong stuff, then dark thoughts can literally swamp you, making it so much harder to function normally. I remember getting so confused about the smallest of things – what t-shirt to wear with my jeans, for example, and many times just collapsing on the bed in a flood of tears at my inability to make a simple decision.

During our great sadness, I found it very powerful to journal and record our journey. Whenever I read or heard a nugget of truth – something for me to hold onto – I would write it down and read back over it when I was feeling low. There are pages and pages in those diaries of incoherent ramblings from a woman in deep pain, but in between there are nuggets of gold. Truths placed right where I needed them. Positive encouragements that could take my day from grey to every shade of colour. Words that took my mind off what I didn't have and brought me into the wide-open space of what I could be grateful for. Words are incredibly powerful, so to write and read ones that will bring peace and respite from our difficulties is well worth the time investment we put into it.

One powerful thing I wrote down that helped me later on, as I sat in despair needing encouragement, was the analogy of pushing a boulder. When the pain and suffering begin, you feel as though you are standing in front of a huge boulder, pushing with all your might but seeing very little movement. This can quickly exhaust you and make you want to give up and walk away. You may try to ignore the boulder, but you can't because it obscures your vision and takes up a huge chunk of your attention. Although I'd had to overcome things in life before, moving blockages out of the way or climbing over them, the boulder was my first real roadblock.

With God's help, after much perseverance, I found that the boulder had moved. I could see the road ahead and I was feeling more positive. Now I am not scared of my boulders. They are forever popping up and trying to block my view, or trying to cause me to stop and give up, but I am stronger now. I know how to move them. I get friends to help me roll them away. I break them up with positive words, so they lose all power and become tiny pebbles. I stand on them to see the view more clearly. Whatever it takes, I can now take control, but it was only reading that nugget of truth that made me sit up and take notice. That's when I realised the boulder had, in fact, moved and no longer dominated my life. Writing can be very therapeutic and healing.

I've already mentioned thankfulness and my mind is set on continuing to get the best out of this life, being grateful for what I do have, not getting hung up on what I don't. Paul spoke about this in the Bible in Philippians 4:11-12, where he writes about having found the secret of contentment in life. He was content whether he had much or little, whether he had food or no food. What not everyone realises is that Paul wrote these words after being beaten and shipwrecked, when he was hungry and cold. This is a man who had suffered greatly but was still able to show gratitude and contentment. This is surely what we should be striving for, rather than money, status and "stuff". Right after these words Paul adds, "…for I can do all things through Christ who gives me strength" which leads me on to the most important part of our healing.

You will have read throughout this book that our faith helped Lindz and I in certain situations in various ways. It really was the backbone of everything that happened. Our faith was stretched, challenged, and broken for a while, but that became the thing that pulled us through, making us stronger, more grateful and more determined than before. I have watched how people suffer with a faith in Jesus Christ and without. The difference is so evident to me and, again, brings gratitude that we chose to dig in and remain faithful even through the hardest of times.

I feel free. I am grateful and feel honoured to have gone through such testing and come out stronger. The greatest difference when faith is involved, is hope. The world doesn't offer a lot of hope, though it may pretend to, with a round of IVF and some kind words. It leads us to endless clinics, doctors, vitamins, pills and forums around the world which claim to offer some form of hope, until the conclusion is not what we paid for, hope is dashed, and dreams are broken further.

But my relationship with God the Father became one of finding freedom and hope right in the middle of despair. I was able to reach out to someone who promises to always be there for us, even if some of our desperate prayers seem to go unanswered. I had to learn, in reality, the meaning of Paul's words that "I can do all things through Christ who strengthens me" and I did so not on my own, but with God's help and in a community of people that I was learning to be vulnerable with.

God sees honing our character as far more important than fulfilling our dreams and desires, or helping us to become successful. The potential we have, to live with nothing except for peace, love and contentment, and be among the happiest people in the world, is truly magical. There is endless data to show us that the opposite is not always true. Many of the richest, most "perfect" looking humans also express deep feelings of hopelessness, dissatisfaction and despair. What is it they are missing? I believe it's a friendship with the God who created them – the One who knows them far more intimately than they know themselves.

This is why I am so determined to help people find their hope. Through my suffering, I feel like I hold some keys to help others be released from theirs. And whether they get to know their creator or not through that process, I just want to be there. To tell those suffering that they are not alone. That I understand how it hurts. To give them hope that the boulder that blocks their view right now will one day move, revealing a beautiful sunrise that will bring light into their darkness. Hold on... because this won't last forever. The flicker of light you can see through that dark, dark tunnel is for you. Keep walking, hold hands with those next to you, tell them when you're stumbling and you will get there, I promise.

The best view comes after the hardest climb.

Finding Help

If you find yourself in a similar situation to the one I describe in this book, or have family or close friends who are walking the same road, I hope you will find the following advice useful. We have touched on some of these areas throughout the book, but here is a summary you can refer to whenever you feel stuck and want to get things back into perspective.

Talking. My husband Lindz said it in his chapter: to talk is a most healing thing. Sit down with someone close to you, who you love and trust. It may feel hard to start a conversation and begin to share all you are going through, but even the smallest admission of the confusion you feel right now will bring you a bit of freedom. Start by sharing something personal and private, that doesn't require advice, just a listening ear. If the person you're talking to has experienced infertility themselves, and you would love to glean some advice from them, that's okay.

If you're reading this because you want to help someone you love who is in this situation, be a great listener and don't try to offer solutions. As well-meaning as it might seem, if you leap in with words of advice rather than simply listening, it can feel to the person as though you are trying to shut them up. It's certainly difficult to know what to say in a situation like this, but remember that the person mainly wants to be heard and understood. People often offered me advice along the lines of, "My cousin's best mate stopped trying altogether, then immediately got pregnant with twins" etc, and probably felt as though they were helping me in some way, but it just made me feel even more alone.

Remember that the person who is suffering is completely loved and precious and their journey is unique to them. Don't throw out any false hope in an attempt to make things better. This is far worse than agreeing with them that the situation is rubbish and hurts like heck. Just love them, listen to them, and speak only to tell them you're sorry what they're going through right now is so darn hard. Remember when I chatted to Jan at the Trafford Centre? I don't recall her saying a single word, but the *love*, oh man! I felt so "seen" because she loved me so well. What a blessing to have friends like that. Aim to be that person for your friend or family member.

Men need to talk too. A video went around on social media recently with a man speaking directly to the camera. He said, "If you ever ask a man how he is doing and he says, 'I'm alright', I'm here to tell you that man is *not* alright. That man is battling demons you cannot even possibly imagine; that man is struggling every single day to find a reason to keep going. And the reason we say we're alright is because, as a man, no one really cares what you're going through, so why even bother to say it? But you know what, I feel you brother, because I'm *alright* too."

I found this short monologue deeply upsetting. Men need to talk too, but often they believe that no one will care, even if they do. Lindz told me that just having a conversation in a pub over a pint really helped him to order his jumbled thoughts. It helped him to normalise the deep pain he was carrying and lose some of that "weight" men can feel, trying to carry both themselves and their partner through the situation. Talk and advice around infertility is so often directed towards women, yet men also battle with incredible insecurities and feelings of failure that are rarely shared. We need to step up for our men. If you think your brother, son, or friend is carrying something that is weighing him down – it could be anything – invite him out for a drink and ask him. Let him know you are there for him and you want to listen. He will probably leave that conversation feeling 10 feet tall, because he will know that someone has seen him; someone cared enough to ask and listen.

Gratitude. I've already spoken about gratitude, but it's so important that here is a reminder. Thankfulness can keep us sane through every season of our life, not just when we're hurting. Every day, seek out something to be grateful for because choosing gratitude over self-pity is a very powerful thing. For me, a walk around a nearby park always helped. I'd look up at the birds, at the blossom on the trees and the cloud formations. Or, on an evening walk, I looked at the stars, which would take my breath away and help me shift my perspective away from the pain.

Undoubtedly, there will always be someone who is worse off than us, and I used to say things like, "At least Lindz is alive" or "at least I haven't loved a child and lost them", telling myself I was blessed not to have suffered more loss that I had. But I don't think that's the best way to access gratitude. Actively choosing something to be grateful for is far more powerful. Choosing to see the beauty around us, being thankful for the roof over our heads, being able to choose what we eat each day, having the freedom to walk, meet others and pray (depending on what country we live in)… these are things we can easily take for granted, but can choose to be grateful for. When we are thankful for even the smallest of things, it can truly lift our hearts and spirits.

Exercise is another big one. My husband and I were both brought up enjoying the outdoors. We would play and picnic, bike ride, horse ride and paddle in any stream we passed. I have a rule that my mum passed on to me, that if we are going down a hill with someone we love, we have to run and shout "Woohoo!" Of course, bystanders find this very amusing, but I can't help myself – it's the law! Lindz and I have built regular exercise into our lives and try to walk anywhere we can, getting outside as much as possible. Exercise is so important to our mental health but when we are suffering it's not always easy to maintain. There was a season where I found it incredibly hard to get motivated to move at all, let alone attend an exercise class. Many people don't see the point of structured exercise, some being proud of the fact they've never set foot in a gym, but its benefits to our mental wellbeing are well known and backed up with plenty of scientific evidence.

Exercise is not a magical healer, but it can help a lot as it depletes our stress hormones. If you are feeling low and lethargic, why not start with a gentle walk around your local park (perhaps avoiding the play areas if it hurts to see children playing). Maybe take a book and find a bench halfway round. Numerous studies have shown that exercising in forests or parks can reduce blood pressure as well as the stress-related hormones cortisol and adrenaline. A short walk or a jog around a park will positively affect your mood, which is just want you need when you are feeling low. Make time for some form of exercise every day, whether it's a quick walk or taking the stairs instead of the lift. You may be a gym bunny and know these benefits already, but if you're not, anything that gets your body moving will blow away some of the cobwebs and sadness.

Journaling is a brilliant way to bring order and clarity to a confused, hurting mind. It helped me no end and I am sure you noticed that I quoted some of my journal entries to help give context to my words. When I look back on them now, I see smudged ink and screwed up pages where I was so angry I would just grab my words and ball them in my fist, or I would cry so hard as I was writing that the letters would merge into one as the ink became wet. But the incredible thing is, when I read those pages again, it was incredibly healing. I saw the girl I used to be and how far I'd come. When I researched whether there were any health benefits to be had from journaling, I found these interesting results…

Writing a journal can help you to stay accountable to the goals you have for your life. If you have things you'd like to achieve or change during this time of waiting, be specific and keep looking back at them to track your progress and keep you motivated. When you start to see any positive change, or ways in which you have coped with certain circumstances, it will help you grow in confidence.

A big benefit of journaling is to reduce stress and anxiety, which is just what we need when going through a challenging situation. Sometimes, negative words and thoughts can go on a loop around our heads, which can make the situation feel even worse. We can break that by writing it all down and releasing those words from our mind. For our general health, journaling can also improve our memory and writing and communication skills. So, you see, it really is worth putting pen to paper when you are feeling overwhelmed.

Laughing is incredibly good for us. We may feel as if laughter has totally removed itself from our lives. Perhaps you feel guilty about laughing when you are carrying such a burden. Yet experiencing laughter – whether by watching a funny TV show with a good friend or playing chase with a young child – can bring a real lightness to our heart and help us forget the dark clouds hanging over us. I used to watch Peter Kay's stand-up tour on DVD a lot as it made me laugh so hard. Find something that works for you, something light and not too dark in its humour, and just let go. Perhaps record in your journal how you felt after a good laugh so that you remember to do it again and again.

Counselling. I remember sitting with an older friend who had taken many people through some very tough times as a counsellor. She was absolutely brilliant at drawing things out of me, finding out my deepest fears and desires, then coming to a natural conclusion. Earlier in this book, I spoke about coming to a crossroads in my journey and having to take the decision to leave BlushUK if I wanted to have children – even though singing and performing was my life. I look back at my younger self and recall the inner turmoil I experienced at that time. A professional counsellor can help you to talk through issues like this and guide you to arrive at the right decisions for you. A good counsellor will not offer any superficial, pat advice but will help you to process your thoughts clearly and see a way forward.

PRAYER. I have written this in capitals as I believe prayer was the main thing that got me through our eight years of waiting. So many types or levels of prayer took place during this time. There were quick prayers in the early stages, deep ones full of angst and desperation, angry ones shouting at and questioning God's "plan". There were the prayers where I surrendered and gave up. Ones where I begged for a while, then fell silent. Then there was my beautiful friend, Lynn, who at that point said, "Right, you've done your bit, now it's my turn. I will lift my arms for you." In other words, she took over for me. It was such a relief to hand it over for a while, to stop torturing myself thinking that having no children meant God wasn't listening or didn't love me. That is certainly NOT the truth. The truth is that Jesus sat or walked with me every step of the way and never left my side. He cried with me, celebrated as I moved through suffering into freedom, laughed with me when I was happy and just held me when I sobbed. I can clearly see this looking back, and millions of other Christians all over the world have said the same – that they felt God heard them more clearly in their pain than their joy. What a comfort! This tells me that prayer works, and is definitely worth pursuing.

Useful contacts

I have read a lot around the subject of infertility and researched charities or ministries who are caring for those going through it. Below is a list of organisations who provide helpful advice, or that you can reach out to. It's not an exhaustive list, but hopefully some of the links will be a help if you would like more information and advice.

www.fertilitynetworkuk.org

This is a very simply written website with clear information about every aspect of infertility, both emotional and scientific. It is very interesting and a great resource.

www.nhs.uk/conditions/infertility

Straight talking and thorough, as you would expect from the NHS.

www.resolve.org

This is a US-based website that talks about helping those walking through infertility to reach a resolution "empowered by knowledge, supported by community, united by advocacy, and inspired to act".

www.sarahs-laughter.com

Sarah's Laughter is a faith-based website which reaches out to all, whether you have a different faith to Christianity or no faith. They aim to help people by connecting them to communities of people going through similar situations, and pray for those who need it. They offer resources and podcasts to help people along their journey.

www.waitinginhopeinfertility.com

The title of this website says it all. It seeks to provide support and hope to those walking through infertility.

www.homeforgood.org.uk/what-the-church-needs-to-know-about-infertility

There is a wonderful article on this website that is predominantly about fostering and adoption. It talks about what the Church (and I believe many people in general) needs to know about infertility, how to look after or speak to those going through it, and far more importantly, what *not* to say!

www.britishfertilitysociety.org.uk

This resource is predominantly about what science can offer the waiting mother or father. It is a very interesting and simple read, making it a great resource if you are choosing to try fertility treatments.

www.seasidesundays.com/movies-about-infertility/

If you are able, have a look for documentaries or films about infertility. There are more and more being made to help people deal with, or make sense of what they are going through. It is also so good to know that you are not alone in this.

https://www.mariposatrust.org/

The Mariposa Trust is a leading support charity primarily working within the field of baby loss and bereavement.

https://www.sayinggoodbye.org/

Saying Goodbye provides comprehensive information, advice, support and much more to anyone who has suffered the loss of a baby, at any stage of pregnancy, at birth or in infancy.

Last word

Thank you so much for reading my book, written from the heart, blood, sweat and tears included! I pray it helps you to feel more empowered to keep moving through "the wait" or to help someone you love to walk their journey in hope, feeling loved and held the whole way.

Lucy x